More Praise for *Pushback*

"*Pushback* performs the service of arming women with the single most compelling career advancement strategy at their disposal: negotiating skills. Rezvani's day-to-day bargaining tactics are simple to apply, yet intensely effective and stunningly powerful."

—**Linda C. Babcock**, Ph.D., James Mellon Walton Professor of Economics, Carnegie Mellon University; coauthor, *Women Don't Ask*

"Any woman who has ever swallowed hard and accepted less than she should at work will benefit from this book. Selena provides a template for negotiating gracefully and powerfully for what you want, need, and deserve."

—**Sally Helgesen**, author, *The Female Vision* and *The Female Advantage*

"You must read Selena's new book, *Pushback*. In an age of intellectual capital where value added is so often subjective, it is absolutely vital for women leaders to highlight their contributions and ask for what they want, and this dynamite book will teach you how to find your own voice and style for effectively self-advocating."

—**Manisha Thakor**, coauthor, *On My Own Two Feet: A Modern Girl's Guide to Personal Finance*

"*Pushback* is a compelling playbook for taking charge. Selena Rezvani nails the personal tools—from negotiating persuasively to thinking strategically—for the leadership of which all managers are capable and on which all firms depend."

—**Michael Useem**, professor of management, director of the Leadership Center, Wharton School, University of Pennsylvania

Pushback

How Smart Women Ask—and Stand Up—for What They Want

Selena Rezvani

Foreword by Lois P. Frankel

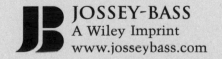

JOSSEY-BASS
A Wiley Imprint
www.josseybass.com

Published by Jossey-Bass
A Wiley Imprint
One Montgomery Street, Suite 1200, San Francisco, CA 94104-4594—www.josseybass.com

Jossey-Bass books and products are available through most bookstores. To contact Jossey-Bass directly call our Customer Care Department within the U.S. at 800-956-7739, outside the U.S. at 317-572-3986, or fax 317-572-4002.

Wiley also publishes its books in a variety of electronic formats and by print-on-demand. Some material included with standard print versions of this book may not be included in e-books or in print-on-demand. If the version of this book that you purchased references media such as a CD or DVD that was not included in your purchase, you may download this material at http://booksupport.wiley.com. For more information about Wiley products, visit www.wiley.com.

Library of Congress Cataloging-in-Publication Data

Rezvani, Selena.
    Pushback : how smart women ask—and stand up—for what they want / Selena Rezvani ;
Foreword by Lois P. Frankel. — First edition.
        pages cm
    Includes bibliographical references and index.
    ISBN 978-1-118-10490-3 (hardback)
    1. Assertiveness (Psychology) 2. Leadership in women. 3. Women executives. I. Title.
    BF575.A85R498 2012
    658.4'09082—dc23
                                                                    2011052577

Printed in the United States of America
FIRST EDITION
HB Printing 10 9 8 7 6 5 4 3 2 1

For my mom

Contents

Foreword

Smart women ask; nice girls just don't get it. The first part of this phrase is part of the subtitle of this book, and the second part is the title of my most recent book, coauthored with Carol Frohlinger. Put them together into one sentence and it tells you a lot about women, negotiating, and the ways in which we sabotage our own best efforts when it comes to getting what is most important to us. Behaving according to the rules you were taught in childhood was appropriate for nice little girls but will never enable you to achieve your adult goals. Nice is necessary for success in any endeavor; it's simply not sufficient.

Case in point. Although I've never met Selena Rezvani, I admired her gumption when she wrote to inquire if I might be willing to provide a foreword for her book. She walked the talk. She asked! And let that be the first of many lessons as you read on. Nice girls just don't get it because they don't ask. Mired in old messages and stereotypes, they long for more—whether that's more respect, money, love, or you name it—but they're hesitant to ask for fear of being labeled too needy, greedy, off-base, insensitive, or a host of other adjectives that are far from the truth. Make no mistake about it. The opposite of a nice girl is not someone who is self-centered, egotistical, or worse—she's a smart woman.

So why do we allow the names we're called when we're assertive, when we ask, and when we stand up for ourselves to wound and immobilize us? Because we live in what Anne Wilson Schaef calls the white male system. By definition a system is designed to perpetuate itself. Think political system, family system, or ecological system.

The name-calling, put-downs, and negative innuendo that result when you advocate for yourself are no more than the system trying to keep you where it thinks you belong. And you know what? Each time you acquiesce to these messages the system has succeeded.

In the form of rock-solid research and advice, *Pushback* offers help in overcoming counterproductive social messages and self-talk. It provides practical strategies that will help you challenge norms and illuminate possibilities you may have never before considered. From negotiating an alternative work arrangement, lobbying for flexibility, or asking for a job that doesn't yet exist, this book delivers news you can immediately use. As a consultant, executive coach, and recovering nice girl, I know how difficult personal change can be. If you knew better, you'd do better. Whether you're the freshest face in your organization or a freshly appointed senior vice president—*Pushback* provides you with knowledge and tools to amplify your success.

As I often tell my clients, no one will ever take better care of you than you will take care of yourself. Not your boss, your partner, your parents, or your friends. As well-meaning and supportive as they may be, when it comes right down to it, no one knows better than you what's right for you. It's a matter of clearing the path to knowing what you do want and don't want, trusting your instincts, and preparing yourself for life's challenges. The power of *Pushback* will help you in all three arenas—and more. You're a smart woman. Now, act like it.

January 2012   Lois P. Frankel, PhD
Pasadena, California   Best-selling author, *Nice
                                  Girls Don't Get the
                                  Corner Office*, *Nice Girls
                                  Don't Get Rich*, and *Nice
                                  Girls Just Don't Get It*

Preface

Wanting a raise or a flexible schedule. Craving the chance to lead a coveted project. Needing to sell others on the value of your ideas. Wanting to be heard in a meeting. Finding yourself saying "yes" when you mean "no."

There are circumstances nearly every day, in every area of life, where we can and need to *push back*—to articulate, advocate for, and hold out for what we want and what is ours. This book is about building the ability to push back in the arena of work. I believe this ability is the foundation for professional success and fulfillment, and that it can be learned.

Why write a book on pushback for women in particular? In my professional life, I have the opportunity to talk to women colleagues, students, and professionals about leadership and negotiation all the time. Since 2007, I've been immersed in the world of leadership development for women. I've had the pleasure of writing a monthly column for the *Washington Post,* where I connect with thousands of women about the journey and passage of becoming a leader. These readers, who are dealing with leadership issues firsthand and are in the trenches, tell it to me straight, explaining exactly what they face in the workplace. I also serve as a commentator on NPR's women's show, *51 Percent,* where I can share with listeners those issues most pressing for women in the business world. I write a blog for Forbes.com on women and careers that provides tactical guidance for a female audience on how to navigate many common yet hard-to-handle workplace dynamics. And I had the good fortune of volunteering for years as a vice president for the National Association of Women MBAs, a group that encourages ambitious young women to lead, regardless of their chosen career path or interests.

Together with my business partner, Jane Weiss, I co-own a consulting practice, where we work with leaders to help them better engage and retain their female workforce, positioning an inclusive workplace as a competitive advantage. Regardless of where these activities take me, I make a point to have conversations with women who are building their careers *right now*. No matter what female audience I speak to—whether it's Johnson & Johnson's corporate women's group, business students at Harvard University, or attendees of an international leadership conference—women tend to ask me the same questions, most often related to negotiation, advocacy, conflict, and standing firm:

- How can I confront a workplace issue head-on without decimating the relationship?
- I understand the value of asking for what I want, but I tend to avoid the "tough conversations." Why is this so difficult and how can I do it anyway?
- I find myself flustered in negotiations, giving in too soon or agreeing to terms on the spot. How can I be more prepared the next time?
- What's the best way to take a firm position when my needs aren't being met or if I disagree?
- I tend to negotiate more often at home than at work. How can I translate these skills to business situations?
- If I want to advocate fervently about an issue, how far should I push?

Given that these questions imply a level of anxiety and discomfort about negotiating, you might wonder whether women are simply born without a "negotiation gene." The simple but certain answer is "no." Yes, for many women, negotiating—among other pushback skills—has all the attraction and appeal of cleaning a litter box, and yet, as I show later in this book, women are actually uniquely positioned to succeed at bargaining conversations. Seeing the power in negotiating can move women from apprehension to strength and authority: for this reason, this book focuses largely on teaching negotiating skills and techniques.

For many women, when we're faced with a less-than-optimal situation or circumstance, there are niggling influences guiding us *not* to act. We might wonder, "Shouldn't I be concerned with what I need, not what I want?" "What if asking for what I want turns 'them' off?" "Is it possible for me to be nice and assertive at the same time?" Our own internal monologue might convince us that nothing can be done, that we're not qualified to ask in the first place, or tempt us to avoid the confrontation altogether. We also might have attempted to negotiate before, only to have our request struck down—a factor that led us to deduce that it's easier to sidestep these conversations than to engage in them and suffer defeat. Our own self-questioning can indeed stop us long before we get to the negotiating table.

I've written this book for every woman who wants to build her pushback skills and reach her career goals, and I believe the techniques and advice given here will help any working woman to claim what she wants and what is hers. In particular, I want to reach women with leadership in their sights. As part of the next generation of women leaders, you are primed to thrive in the work world—finally assuming the high-level positions in which women have historically had a nonpresence. You certainly don't lack drive or ambition. In fact you hold unprecedented power—outnumbering men in the workforce,[1] garnering more advanced degrees than men,[2] and controlling more than half of the world's overall wealth.[3] Women's opportunities today would no doubt be unrecognizable to many of our grandmothers and great-grandmothers.

And yet, the job environments that greet you are not yet truly gender inclusive. The policies and structures that you navigate will be largely man-made. You may have a few high-ranking role models you can relate to but your work culture may feel stifling. Even the benefits extended to you will largely undermine the realities many of you face such as motherhood or the quest for a life outside of work. To be sure, the work world needs "work," and you're the perfect candidate to change it. If we as women are going to build on the unmatched power and momentum we have today, *we'll* need to lead the charge. If we want our voices to be heard and to be part of the everyday decision making that affects us, *we'll* need to keep pushing back.

Luckily, the conditions are lush; the setting and timing are just right. Beyond the fact that women represent a compelling talent pipeline, the world requires feminine leadership like never before. I would contend that women's greater abilities to *include, empower, empathize, stabilize, glean,* and *lead* are direly needed in a job market, corporate culture, and economy that are struggling.

You represent the new face of women leaders and role models in the making. By setting your sights high, you will avoid the syndrome that leaves so many people ailing from uncontested, low expectations. Come be a part of asking for what you want and need—in fact, be a leader.

The goal of this book is to offer you a better approach to getting what you want. Based on leadership theory, negotiating strategy, and psychological questioning, combined with the firsthand lessons and experiences of women executives, the chapters that follow can serve as a roadmap for helping you attain your own goals, whatever they may be. My interviews with women executives at the top strata of their fields taught me much about the many forms of pushback, its power, and applications for using these skills every day. These women's insights changed and strengthened me profoundly, and I hope they will do the same for you by helping you to find your own pushback voice, style, and signature abilities.

1

Why Push Back?

Last fall, I stood before hundreds of women, presenting a workshop on negotiation skills. The scene was the Pennsylvania governor's conference for women, an event that brings together 4,500 women from around the world, with the aim of promoting gender balance in leadership and facilitating rousing debates, discussions, and learning. The promise of my session was similar to that of this book: to give attendees techniques to maneuver through tough bargaining conversations—techniques they could use in all areas of their lives.

The women who attend this conference are extremely bright—most hold advanced degrees and are very successful professionally. They are also engaged, vocal, and motivated when it comes to shaping the trajectory of their careers. Kicking off the session, I asked the question, "Who in this room counteroffered when negotiating your current salary?" About 10 percent of the women raised their hands.

This picture was uniquely unsettling but not unique. It's representative of women's behavior when negotiating—and not just about salary. According to the research of Carnegie Mellon's Linda Babcock and Sara Laschever, women report "a great deal of apprehension" about negotiation at a rate 2.5 times more than men.[1]

How is it possible that in the year 2012—when there are more women than men in the workforce[2] and women earn more degrees than men[3]—women are still apprehensive about negotiating? After all, we negotiate every day in countless ways. We bargain with our children and partners, making almost daily trades and concessions of our time. We demand a refund on a broken stroller, negotiate with our bosses to ensure coverage while we're on vacation, or ask the hotel maître d' for a room further away from the elevator. We're in bargaining situations all the time. Yet, time and again, my female colleagues, students, and friends tell me resoundingly, "I hate negotiating and I'm no good at it."

WOMEN LEADERS GET THERE BY ASKING

When researching my first book, I spoke with thirty women executives about how they own and use their power at work. I learned that successful women ask for what they want; I even dedicated a full chapter of that book to the art of asking. The women executives I convened figured out through experience that doing good work does not guarantee rewards. They learned that people who are vocal and advocate on their own behalf move up, not those who wait to be noticed. In interviewing them, I also learned that women who achieve leadership status challenge long-standing beliefs. They push back on the "good-girlisms" with which they grew up: "be seen and not heard," "always be nice," and "don't be too outspoken." They don't take "no" as a final, damning answer, nor do they allow rejection to create a deeply personal wound. On the contrary, to survive in a top role, women executives ask for what they want. They're firm. They don't accept what's unacceptable. They speak and maneuver with power.

To understand how women leaders achieve this level of savvy, I sought out even more specific data, turning to a new set of twenty women leaders in the top echelons of their fields. I had the pleasure of sitting down with these women in hour-long mentoring sessions, to hear in their own words about the learning, mistakes, observations, and successes they'd experienced with self-advocacy.

I started each interview by defining the term *pushback* to be certain we had the same foundation of understanding. The word is often used to mean resistance. I explained that I was using it rather more broadly—and more positively. In the context of those interviews and of this book, *pushback* represents the group of skills that allow us to take a stand, be firm, or advocate on our own behalf. It also encompasses our adeptness at advancing a cause, making a request, and persuading others of the merits of our view. We can use it to go after what we want, and we can use it to defend what is ours and what we need.

We're called on to push back when

- We're asked to chair an event. We want to say "no" but our reflex is to answer "yes."
- We're told that there are two paths for advancement at our job: option A and option B. We're interested in the nonexistent option C.
- We're interested in expanding our small business internationally and we'll need to get our business partners, all of whom are satisfied with the status quo, onboard.
- We've had a strong year at work, hitting all of our targets, but we've just been notified we'll be receiving a 2.5 percent raise.
- We're shuttling our kids to their fifth doctor appointment in two months and fuming that we don't share this responsibility with our partner.
- We're being talked down to in a meeting, when in fact we have a master's degree in the subject at hand and ten years' experience in the field.
- We spend $250 on a long-anticipated meal for a special occasion, only to experience an evening of rude waitstaff and cold soup.
- We've just been assigned another administrative project when what we really want is to manage a client account.

Self-Advocacy Matters Everywhere

A study of 136 women receiving care at an ultrasound clinic examined women's beliefs about their role in medical encounters with their physicians. Women who reported repeating information when they felt their doctors did not hear them, asking their doctors to explain information they did not understand, or reminding their doctors about screening tests were more likely to receive needed diagnostic tests than those who reported using these assertive behaviors less often. Interestingly, women who behaved assertively were more likely to view physicians as advisors in their health care and less likely to view their physicians as experts.[4]

Pushback is not always a formal process, as you can see from the previous examples. Sometimes a simple switch in the way we view our role can be action enough to drive a negotiation or debate in a favorable direction. Seeing the other person in a nondeferential and a more equal, peer-to-peer way can also make all the difference in getting the outcomes we want. What's more, pushback is not always about a grand issue or dealt with on a large scale. Each scenario, large or small, requires similar skills. If you're tackling a negative experience with a maître d' or looking to challenge your boss, you'll need a firm voice, you'll want to be ready for a different range of reactions, and you'll have to be crystal clear about your main message. It's important to know where you won't give an inch and where you're open to considering alternatives and options or hearing their side. Ratchet this up to the top level—to Middle East peace negotiations, let's say—and you'll find that our world's leaders have to summon a similar mind-set. Pushback skills, you see, can be called on by anyone, anywhere, in any debate situation.

In my interviews for this book, I asked women questions about preparing for negotiations—navigating and communicating one's way through them. I asked how they physically carried themselves in a tough conversation. I asked about the nuts and bolts of pushback how-to and about the inside dish—the stuff no one tells you about in the corporate world but that you need to know in order to thrive in it. I learned about how to gain self-worth, how to engage in office politics positively, and how engaging allies can drive the outcome of a pushback situation. I also queried the women about how they manage relationships after a tough conversation or when they're called on to hold repeated negotiations with the same person.

What caught my attention most in analyzing my data was the answer to a numerical question. I asked these women leaders, "Assuming a woman's career success equals 100 percent, what percentage is accounted for by her effectiveness in negotiating and pushing back?" Of the twenty responses I heard, the answer was compelling. The executives I met with felt, on average, that a full 60 percent of a woman's career success hinges on her pushback skills. One interviewee said, "Pushback and being firm is a large part of your career. You have to operate like you're a shareholder and like you own the company." Although technical skills, academic or business pedigree, and people skills are necessities for those who want to lead, command of your own voice and ability to advocate, according to successful women executives, ranks higher. You can assess for yourself how important pushback is in your particular industry and work environment, but the longer you spend in the corporate world, the more you'll find that 60 percent figure to be rather convincing.

After interviewing more than fifty women executives in writing my columns and books, instead of seeing negotiating and other pushback skills as one part of women owning their power at work, I've come to see it as the *most* important tool at women's disposal. What's more, it's a tool that the top women leaders I interviewed developed through practice. By committing to the art of asserting themselves and taking risks, these successful women became skilled at learning to negotiate, advocate, stand firm, and push back. And so can you. This book will show you how.

WOMEN'S DISTASTE FOR NEGOTIATING

How is it that so many women survive professionally without asking for what they want? Negotiation, after all, can make the difference between getting by and flourishing. In their research, Linda Babcock and Sara Laschever made an interesting discovery: women often experience negotiating passively—something that is being done to them—whereas men see themselves as an active participant in a strategic pursuit. As part of their research, they asked women and men to pick metaphors that they associate with the practice of negotiating. Women most often selected "going to the dentist," and men more often chose "a ballgame" or "a wrestling match."[5] This finding demonstrates, in a painfully clear way, that women not only think of negotiating as a passive experience, but also as uncomfortable as getting a cavity fixed.

Women hesitate to negotiate and push back for many reasons. Chief among them, I would argue, is a relentless—and often subconscious—belief that relationship should trump outcome or agenda. For example, let's say that Janelle, a twenty-eight-year-old junior account manager, is passed over to lead an important new project at work. She is inclined to protest or try to change her boss's mind but doubts quickly start to creep in. How might pushing back change the existing relationship between her and her boss? "What if I'm laughed at, belittled, challenged, or disregarded?" she wonders. The damage, it seems to Janelle, could be irreparable, and is thus not worth the risk.

A second common reason why women shy away from self-advocacy is a paralyzing need for perfect conditions. We are often plagued by misgivings that emanate from the seductively simple questions, "What if I'm wrong?" or "What if I'm not ready?" Both men and women face uncertainty and doubts, to be sure, but men tend to handle this predicament differently than women do. Research shows that in self-assessments, men tend to overestimate their abilities and women commonly underestimate theirs. Take for example a study conducted internally by Hewlett-Packard. The IT giant noticed that women incumbents were applying for internal job openings much less frequently than their male counterparts. Leaders commissioned a study to learn more, and what they found was revealing. Although men noted that they would respond to a job posting if they met 60 percent of the requirements, women would only apply for open jobs if they thought they met 100 percent of the criteria listed. Similarly, banking company Lloyds TSB found that although female employees were 8 percent more likely than men to meet or exceed performance expectations, they tended not to apply for promotions.[6] Often we women feel we have to achieve perfection, that we need *all* of the answers—along with guaranteed outcomes—in order to take a risk (even though risk involves taking action *without* total certainty).

Raising our hands then, either as participants or as resisters, can feel like an impossibly loaded affair. If we must seamlessly maintain our relationships while getting every fact and figure exactly right—if we are insistent on "victory or bust"—no wonder we don't want to ask for what we want!

THE COST OF NOT ASKING FOR WHAT WE WANT

Pushing past our discomfort with advocacy, risk, and negotiating, however, is critical for our success. Negotiations are among the most materially significant dealings we have in our personal lives, and they are particularly important at work. What other conversations create value, drive growth, or increase monetary profit at the same rate? When we hesitate to ask for what we want, it substantially hurts our earning potential, our access to plum work assignments, and our opportunities for promotions. From a broader perspective, not asking for what we want limits our input in decisions that affect us, making our voice a barely audible whisper. Not asking encourages us to accept what is, to consent to that with which we disagree, and to leave a world of opportunity unclaimed.

Take Fatima, a thirty-seven-year-old accountant, who had to decide whether or not she wanted to take a particular job. Fatima was being courted by a local firm with a good reputation. She liked the people she'd interviewed with, her commute to work would be shortened by taking this job, and she felt comfortable and at ease in the work culture the company fostered. The job seemed a clear improvement over her last position, and promised to come with a talented swath of colleagues and a boss who was hands-off. There was only one issue: she wouldn't get paid quite as much as she was making at her current job.

Although she was bothered by her current fate of being perpetually strapped financially, Fatima nonetheless accepted the job. Six months later, she put her finger on an uncomfortable thought. She felt a perceptible resentment toward herself and the company. She was working hard, delivering what she was supposed to, and yet she complained, "I feel like I'm being taken. I'm giving a lot, but not getting much in return when it comes to money." She griped at home—and to anyone else who'd listen—about how she wasn't being paid fairly.

You can imagine Fatima's bitterness when, while having lunch with Rachel, a newly hired accountant, she excitedly told Fatima she was able to negotiate a much more favorable salary than the last job she'd held. Incredulous, Fatima demanded, "How did you do it?!"

"I just asked for it," said Rachel breezily.

Fatima paid too much for not pushing back on her salary offer. Not only did she acquiesce to continuing to live with money worries, her resentment negatively affected her relationship with her new employer from day one and gave her unneeded mental stress. The funny thing about asking is that when we get used to living *without* doing it, any semblance of negotiating becomes as uncomfortable as, say, wearing burlap undergarments. We funnel our discomfort into unproductive and unsatisfying channels: we grumble about our problem to everyone *except* the person who can do something about it. We lambast ourselves for not having the nerve to protest. We are disgusted at how far we'll go to avoid a confrontation altogether. And we may think back disappointedly to a time when we caved, capitulating way too easily with a smile and a "yes," when what we really wanted to say was "no" (I've certainly had this experience).

Deciding whether or not to negotiate or advocate is part of something larger—our conditioning. Animal trainers know a thing or two about the effects of habituation. Elephant trainers, for example, tie baby elephants to poles, and the babies can't get loose no matter how they resist and tug. As the elephants grow and develop to massive proportions and great power, however, they don't realize that they can easily free themselves. So as full-grown adults, they don't even bother trying to escape. Similarly, our assessment of our own power, whether right or wrong, drives the action we're willing to take.

Many of us might recall a pushback situation in which we didn't feel the slightest bit powerful. We then attach that feeling to a sense of what we deserve and who we are in the long term. So we don't ask for what we want, and we never get to challenge our deep-seated thoughts of inadequacy, which means we never get to prove them wrong! And so the cycle continues. At the same time, the effect of experience can work in quite an opposite way. By taking action and practicing the thing we're afraid of, we can give ourselves wins that show us we have power and can use it, leading to a virtuous cycle.

Ironically, as uncomfortable as the thought of asking for what we want is, living without negotiating—without insisting on mutually positive terms—is much tougher than advocating your case. Another irony is that our relationships are actually strengthened when we let the other person know what we want and where we stand. Everything from the conditions of our work, to the projects we take on, to the deadlines to which we agree, is negotiable. Our career prospects can be greatly accelerated when we advocate for what we want and, by the same principle, can be heavily weighed down and stalled by inaction. If you're trying to navigate from point A to point B, wouldn't you prefer a high-powered, state-of-the-art propeller boat as opposed to an oarless rowboat? Indeed, between pushing back and not pushing back, there's no contest.

PUSHBACK AND ECONOMIC POWER

If you're reluctant to ask for what you want, consider that the tangible costs of not negotiating are many. By omitting negotiation from salary discussions, for example, a woman stands to lose more than $1,000,000 over the course of her life compared to a man.[7]

It's been demonstrated that men and women tend to perceive and value money differently. For example, in a national workplace study conducted by LLuminari, Inc., a health education company, researchers found men value pay, money, and benefits, as well as power, authority, and status significantly more than women.[8] Conversely, Lois Frankel, author of *Nice Girls Don't Get Rich*, notes that women value friends and relationships, recognition and respect, communication, fairness and equity, collaboration, and family and home life more than men. Women are encouraged to save money for emergency situations and to spend largely on items to benefit their families, whereas men are often socialized to enlarge their pot of money—to grow and invest it. Women often see money negotiations as tied to their deservingness and what is "fair," whereas men are motivated to negotiate based on what they want.[9]

According to Michael J. Silverstein, Kate Sayre, and John Butman, coauthors of *Women Want More*, women control nearly $20 trillion of the world's spending power, a share that is expected to increase to $28 trillion by 2013.[10] Even so, the fact that we generally earn less than men increases—and amplifies—our financial dependence on them. With half of all marriages ending in divorce, our own share of earning becomes even more of a vitally important lifeline. What's more, the National Committee on Pay Equity found that since the passage of the Equal Pay Act in 1963, women's wages have risen at a molasses-slow rate; less than a half-penny per year.[11] Indeed, as my mentor and top woman leader, Gail Evans, has been known to say, "A man is not a financial plan."

Women also live longer than men, which means, according to financial expert Manisha Thakor, author of *On My Own Two Feet*, we are the ones literally left holding the purse. With less earnings than men, and a tendency to let males take care of bills and savings, the stability of our retirements become endangered.[12] Consider too that over a lifetime women spend an average of twenty-seven years in the workforce, whereas men will spend almost forty years. According to advocacy and education group WISER (Women's Institute for a Secure Retirement), women leave the labor force to have children and care for family members, which means that women retirees receive about half the pension benefits retired men can count on.[13] That means that as a group we are already at an economic disadvantage compared to men, even before we account for the wage disparity between the sexes.

More than any other group, we women need to push back when it comes to getting paid fairly for our work. "What if asking for more money makes me look greedy?" and "What if my number-one priority isn't money?" you might ask. Being paid fairly isn't about being greedy or opportunistic. It's about claiming what's rightfully yours. It's about expecting to have discussions around such matters as money and benefits to reach a mutually beneficial agreement. It's about not assuming you'll be taken care of by outer forces or automatically looked after.

When we negotiate and speak up about what we want, we give our bosses and peers the opportunity to meet our needs or remedy our problem. By not asking managers for the client accounts, leadership opportunities, or visible projects that we want to be part of, we deny them and ourselves the rewards of direct, honest communications. A similar dynamic exists with something else of great import to us: our time. When we see ourselves as able, active negotiators, we consider the flexibility of our schedules, for example, to be a perfectly normal focus of conversation with our manager.

If you're suffering mercilessly day in and day out with a one-and-a-half hour commute, ask yourself, like so many of us need to, if you've done all you can to come up with alternatives and advocate for them. If you have a family, then you might be like many women who have ended up as the primary breadwinners in their household as a result of the economic downturn. Having a less-than-ideal work arrangement can have a direct bearing on the comfort level of our and our family's future. In fact, with all of our advances and modern amenities, the U.S. employment policies continue to be outdated and structured in a way that disadvantages women and their families. For example, we have one of the least generous maternity leave policies in the world, ranking among five countries that do not require employers to offer employees a form of paid maternity leave. According to a study by McGill University's Institute for Health and Social Policy, the United

States, Lesotho, Liberia, Papua New Guinea, and Swaziland were the only countries out of 173 assessed that did not guarantee any paid leave for mothers. Most of the countries studied offer mothers fourteen or more weeks of paid leave.[14] What's more, studies show that when women leave the workforce to have children, they reenter faced with few choices, inflexible boundaries, and perceived workplace penalties, often resulting in depression and pessimism.

It is true that inequity—and even sexism—still exists in corporate America, keeping women from reaching parity in pay, benefits, and top positions at our companies. At the same time, many of us give in to our own aversion to negotiating, advocacy, and pushback, which results in us losing a great deal of our power: power to change our own situation for the better, power to help advocate for someone else, *and* power to reshape the business landscape so that the glass ceiling disappears. Certain external barriers may indeed exist but let's insist that we won't play a role in adding to these inequities. What was true in the past still rings true today: not asking for what is ours and for what we want devastates our potential as women.

YOUNG WOMEN AND PUSHBACK

If you are a young woman at the beginning of your career, you will be just as challenged to confront the current state of the workplace, which includes largely male-made, male-driven corporate cultures. Women of your generation, Gen Yers, are known for placing a high value on independence, on achieving personal goals, and doing things on their own terms.

Yet research shows that despite their hopes and ambition, young women still see limitations. An Accenture study, for example, finds that young, working female millennials (ages twenty-two to thirty-five years old) cite a number of gender-related barriers to their current and future careers, including the pay scale for women (30 percent), a corporate culture that favors men (28 percent), general stereotypes (26 percent), daycare availability (24 percent), lack of women in the top echelons of their organization (20 percent), and obstacles from wanting to start a family (20 percent).[15] It's up to Gen Yers to see that limitations are often the perfect proving ground for negotiating for something better.

To be sure, the next generation of women leaders are the most educated, worldly, multitasking group yet. As such, most of you are looking for hybrid opportunities that allow you to crosspollinate your work and outside interests, integrating your professional *and* personal lives. More than any generation before you, a full 85 percent of you plan on remaining in the workforce after having children.[16]

The impression working boomer moms have left on you is significant. Economist Sylvia Ann Hewlett and her team conducted research examining that intersection in *Bookend Generations.* Sixty-two percent of Gen Y women surveyed by Hewlett confirmed that they don't want to emulate their mothers' "extreme" careers, which involved long hours. If family is going to be a priority, it is felt, the costs of extreme work are simply too great.[17]

You may feel a clear discomfort mimicking workaholic parents, but those of you who had stay-at-home mothers don't necessarily want that path either. Hewlett found that boomers' black-or-white vision of work—opt in and go full throttle or opt out and never have a career—is too constricting a philosophy for Gen Y women. Instead, the youngest female workers tend to give equal emphasis to family and career.

As young women, you are well poised to demand upgrades to the modern workplace. However, Gen Yers will be welcomed by workplaces that are more demanding—not less so—in terms of hours and performance. What's more, Americans today are working more hours per week than in previous years, upping their face time in a culture of "do more with less." Although Gen Yers' vision may be a needed one, a rift between them and employers is certain, and it will be worsened by younger workers not advocating their needs.

But as you maneuver through the first half of your career, you may find that the workplace—and the rigid limitations it imposes, particularly on women—are sobering and disappointing. Much of what women in your generation want for themselves doesn't yet exist. If you want a career custom-built on your own terms, you *must* become a savvy negotiator. And although many Generation Y women might not be inclined toward established leadership positions, those of you who pursue them will need the ability to push and then to push back if your needs and those of your peers are rejected. Self-advocacy, particularly to push for unprecedented terms, will be essential to thrive in a work environment that's still fairly unyielding and largely built for noncaretakers.

What's more, much ado has been made about the dearth of women in substantive leadership roles in government, corporate America, and the nonprofit sector. We need to change these ratios. Whether you are just starting your career or you are well established, asking for what you want can grant you access to top jobs you never thought you could have.

When we don't push back, the effects cascade beyond us. We model for younger women and girls who mimic us—the younger sister who looks up to you with pride and awe as you graduate from an MBA program or your young subordinate who learns about leadership by watching you at work—that it's okay to accept the unacceptable. We demonstrate in the most compelling of ways—through our actions—that speaking up is a liability. If you can't get excited about pushback for your own sake, then call on your concern for others, your entire generation, and the generation that comes after yours. Think about the legacy you are leaving with every action or inaction you take.

WOMEN AND NEGOTIATING—A NATURAL FIT

As I mentioned previously, many women don't like negotiating and may think they're no good at it. But the good news is that women are innately strong negotiators. You might not have gotten that impression from the various leadership training programs for women that, although well-intentioned, often suggest implicitly that women need fixing. Somehow the message those programs seem to communicate is that when it comes to negotiating men have got it right, and that women, inferior and lacking, need educating to learn what they're missing.

I believe otherwise. I believe that women are not deficient. We possess every intellectual tool—and then some—needed to negotiate. In some ways, women have even more bargaining chips than men when you consider, for example, that they earn the majority of advanced degrees today. Similarly, women's collective leadership skill set turns out to be the ideal complement for modern business, lending a collaborative, team-centric management approach to traditionally transactional business dealings. Women have traits that make negotiations into conversations, for example, our ability to see someone's discomfort or need to save face.

Dr. Daniel Goleman points out in his research that technical intelligence is less of a success indicator than we originally thought. Emotional intelligence—the process of recognizing our own feelings and those of others—accounts for a far larger piece of what is required to lead. In his book *Working with Emotional Intelligence,* Goleman notes, "Women, on average, tend to be more aware of their emotions, show more empathy, and are more adept interpersonally [than men]."[18] Reading emotions, it turns out, is a critical success tactic in negotiations, helping a person to quickly pivot, change an approach, or distinguish which issues need to be brought to the surface and further explored.

Additionally, when women negotiate, they tend to do so in a consultative way, meaning that they approach the conversation inquisitively, aiming to understand and solve a problem together with a counterpart (think *us versus the problem* rather than *me versus you*). Women excel at asking diagnostic, or deepening, questions when they need more information, a maneuver that gives a negotiator the instant benefit of more information. This consultative approach tends to put people at ease, builds rapport, and can translate to an advantage. The ability to empathize also can create a relationship where there was formerly none, allowing a woman to gain trust and avoid ego-fueled duels.

Rather than approaching negotiating as a simple business matter, a woman will often build rapport first, asking questions and getting clarity, and push her own agenda second. This way, nuances that were under the surface can come to the forefront and counterparts can be better understood and dealt with. Powerfully, this same collaborative model serves women excellently as negotiators.

Once we get to the negotiating table, women have every opportunity to succeed, outside of our own distaste for self-advocacy and potential conflict, that is. That's precisely why we need a different negotiation mind-set to help us get over the hump. As someone who once pictured negotiation unenthusiastically (think bloody bullfight where someone's going to end up half-dead), I have come to think of it as one exquisitely simple process: a conversation that ends in agreement. This win-win model of negotiating is the one I'll be teaching in this book—it's in line with the stories and insights shared by the women executives I interviewed, it's a good fit with the skills and affinities many women already possess, and it works. Getting clear on why we're asking, knowing that we deserve a seat at the table, and recognizing that our case is worth pursuing are actions that free us to advocate and negotiate from a position of real power.

A FOUR-STEP MODEL OF NEGOTIATION

One of the best investments you'll make in your career is spending time learning a reliable and effective system for negotiation. As you build your skills and learn the art of negotiating, you'll begin to see it not just as a one-time or occasional (and somehow mysterious) transaction but as an everyday necessity. After all, when it comes to daily workplace matters, the question is not *whether* you will have to deal with change, negotiate, or push back accordingly—it's *when* and *how*.

Over the years, I've developed a system for negotiating that is repeatable and adaptable to numerous situations. In the chapters that follow, I will lay out that system and show you how you can apply it and trust it to work. The model has four steps. I'll spend a chapter on each, teaching a mixture of skill-building, strategy, and in-the-moment techniques, so that by the end you will have a box of tools and be well on your way to mastering their use. The last chapter of the book steps back to view a bigger picture, exploring some of the ways the skills of workplace negotiating, advocating, and pushback can further your larger ambitions and goals.

Here are the steps of a thorough, complete, well-conducted negotiation process; you'll notice that more than half of the work takes place before you even sit down at the table.

Step One: Prepare Psychologically

Understanding our own feelings, disposition, strengths, weaknesses, and style is an often overlooked or deemphasized part of the negotiation process but self-understanding can help you better regulate your demeanor during an actual negotiation, among other benefits. If negotiations feel confrontational or uncomfortable to you, understanding the roots of your discomfort with negotiating and pushing back can clear the fog and allow for forward movement. Having a good picture of your existing strengths and style can help you identify different strengths to build up and new styles to try on, adding to your repertoire of skills.

Step Two: Do Your Homework

Successful women who have become particularly adept at pushing back always do their homework. They work to be the most informed and smartest in the room when it comes to the facts. I will show you how to leverage different levels of information, from data, to opinions, to the environmental and social factors, that buoy support for your cause. This step also involves sussing out your counterpart's driving forces, temperament, and style; preparing the way for the main conversation by soliciting input from other people; crafting a compelling story out of all the data you've gathered; and choosing your style, time, and turf.

Step Three: Maneuver Through the Conversation

Preparing—internally and by doing your homework on your subject and your counterpart—is fine and good but you will demonstrate your true abilities when you steer your way through a real negotiation. Managing yourself in the middle of a tough conversation can be tricky but there are many effective strategies and tactics for navigating it, including the art of making concessions and of dealing with a range of agreeable, dismissive, or even combative partners, the use of what I call *deepening* questions, and the strategic uses of silence.

Step Four: Follow Up

This chapter will cover two different kinds of follow-up practiced by the best negotiators. One is internal, involving reflection on how the conversation went: which techniques were used (on both sides of the table) and how effective they were, and what factors went into your success (or lack of success, sometimes). This kind of calm, thorough, inquisitive assessment after the fact is a powerful practice for boosting your skills. The other kind of follow-up is really the final step in the negotiating conversation itself. Once you've finalized a negotiation—whether it's a conversation with your boss about getting assigned to a plum project or advocating for one of your ideas—it is critical to view the negotiation as incomplete and still in process. Summarizing the terms that were discussed is an underestimated step of negotiating, and it allows you to protect yourself by making clarifications as needed and minimizing misunderstandings between you and the other party. I will show you strategies to safeguard agreements in writing and verbally, and I'll share with you the importance of maintaining the relationship with your counterpart and your own reputation for professionalism, no matter how the negotiation goes.

SHOOT FOR THE MOON

The pushback skills of negotiation and advocacy aren't just two of several leadership competencies. They're the most important tools at a woman's disposal. A woman can work on being well networked or technically brilliant, but without the ability to skillfully ask for what she wants, she has nothing.

Negotiating and advocating are skill sets you will call on during the length of your career—and they involve skills you can begin building now, starting right where you are. Using exercises, structured advice, and the wisdom and insight of a score of women leaders who've walked the road before you, this book will help you prepare for negotiations by understanding your own emotions and style, building a case, preparing to meet your counterpart, navigating tough conversations, and following up. I wrote this book to get you thinking, reflecting, and most of all shifting from where you are to where you want to be.

You see, negotiating on your own behalf is about far more than getting a material good. It's about having a voice, piping up, and advocating for yourself. As you strengthen your muscles of self-agency, a whole new world of possibilities will open up. Beyond simply asking more often for what you want and what is rightfully yours, you'll ignite a deep, healthy self-respect. Your strength may even astonish you.

2

Find Your Pushback Style

I f there was ever a time for women to push back, it's now. We are frequently in situations that require versatile, extemporaneous negotiation skills. And I don't mean the once-a-year raise type of negotiation, I mean the everyday kind. Consider that we're getting married (and divorced), buying homes, relocating, starting businesses, and moving into the executive ranks in unprecedented numbers. More women than men, by a sizeable margin, are single parents acting as heads of households. And as it turns out, we're the largest, most bankable talent pipeline: women make up more than half of the U.S. labor force.[1]

Despite some of our gains, women continue to make up a meager portion of senior leaders in government, business, and even in those fields that are female dominated. Our low presence in top decision-making roles diminishes our contributions, gives us little say in corporate and societal directions, and reduces us to mere observers.

Yet, our own perceptions about the act of negotiating may indeed be the most pivotal lever of change. Deborah Simpson, chief financial officer of The Boston Consulting Group, made a key observation: "Women don't seem to value money in the same way that men do, which means we may lean less on the skills of advocacy and negotiation." Be that as it may, we can still transpose skills from one area of life to another. "Don't segment your negotiating so much," says Darlene Slaughter, VP and chief diversity officer at

Fannie Mae. "Recognize all the times you're negotiating outside of work, whether shopping, with your kids, or purchasing a car. Don't put yourself in a box. You have plenty of skills you use off the job so don't say, 'I'm not a negotiator.'" Adds DeeDee Wilson, SVP of finance at L.L.Bean, "Try not to have negotiations but instead have conversations that lead to a good middle ground. As women we say we hate to negotiate. Well don't negotiate then! Go in and dialogue until you find an agreement."

The opportunities—and the need—to negotiate are simply everywhere. What's more, you will find yourself in many unanticipated bargaining situations—ones in which you have the upper hand powerwise and ones in which you're negotiating with those over whom you have zero authority. Most likely in your lifetime you will ask for things from people you like, maybe even love, and from people you detest. You'll experience what it's like to negotiate for something casually and you'll learn what happens when you carefully prepare. If you dare, you'll take the time to develop your own style of advocating so that you can easily answer, "Who will I be when it's time to push back?"

Trust Your Gut

When do you know it's time to stand up, push back, and advocate? Of all the things we will look at together in this book, that part is easiest. Throughout your life, you will consistently hear, from the most reliable sources, what is worthy of pushback. Your own wisdom will alert you, telling you that something needs to be done. It might emerge as an internal nudge, a tingle—even the lump in your throat might be signaling to you that "I don't feel all is right about this."

Our gut instinct always leaves us clues. When something has rubbed you the wrong way, it may surface as general discomfort, anger, or frustration—even dread. You might get off the phone as many of us do, thinking bitterly, "I just agreed to more than I wanted to. How did that happen?!" Indeed, you may course with resentment while you find some well-suited, four-letter descriptors for the person who just "pushed you around." Not until reflecting on the incident later in the day do you think, "I should've pushed back."

On Listening to Your Gut

"I left Nike as a divisional CFO for the opportunity to become the CFO of a small, rapidly growing retailer. After almost two years, I recognized that the work I loved doing and the goals I had for the role were not consistent with what was needed. In the end, as much as I loved the company and the people there, it really wasn't the right job for me. I looked at the situation and realized I could stick with it or recognize the situation for what it was. I worked with the CEO and the Private Equity partners to exit the company without putting them in a bind. That was a big risk since I left without another job lined up in the middle of a recession."

—DeeDee Wilson, SVP of finance at L.L.Bean

There are moments when all of us miss our own internal heeding. Yet there's no other person, book, or resource that can do the job of our own instincts. Learning to listen to our deepest preferences, and especially pondering them *before* acting, may be our very best recourse. Susan McFarland, executive vice president and principal accounting officer at Capital One, says, "My gut is consistently smarter than my brain. If something is nagging at you, then there's usually something to it. . . . Have one good night between a situation confronting you and you confronting the situation. One night leads to a world of clarity."

Your instinct will tell you where it sits on an issue, and it's up to you to pay attention to that information. Many avenues exist for getting better at listening to your gut instinct and then using that information to your best advantage. Here are some questions to ask yourself that will help you build your awareness of what your gut instinct is telling you about an issue. You can use them in any situation, practicing getting in touch with your instinct even when the issue at hand is trivial.

- Will I have regrets if I do or don't act in some way on this? If I suspect I will have regrets, what are they?
- What should I do? (Listen to the first answer that comes into your mind.)
- Imagining I'm ten years older than I am, how would the "older me" counsel the "younger me" on this issue?
- What is the cost of not acting on this issue? What are the potential gains of moving forward?
- What would I tell my best friend to do in this situation?

Another method for getting at your own best wisdom is to meditate. Take five minutes to sit quietly, stilling your mind. Clearing out all mental debris, ask yourself where you stand on the issue you're grappling with at the end of the five minutes.

Some people see their trusty gut instinct as simply their own deepest urgings. Others may view it more analytically. "Much of what you think of as 'your gut' is experience you've built up over time," suggests Sheila Murphy, associate general counsel at MetLife. "That experience allows you to make reliably good, quick decisions. Keep exposing yourself to varied experiences and your instincts will steer you the right way." Sheila underscores the idea that we each have a ready archive of information, just waiting to be accessed; she also suggests that when we take action and open ourselves to experience, our instincts (which are built on experience) increase their scope of effectiveness.

YOUR BODY OF KNOWLEDGE

Using our instincts as the catalyst to push back, like many skills, is something we get better at doing over time. Another powerful source of data is our bodies, which are audaciously good readers of pushback situations and give us all kinds of cues we can learn to become aware of.

Take Noelle, who is in a contentious conversation with her manager, disagreeing about which new employee to hire in a key departmental role. She's been overridden before but in this situation *she knows* she's right. As Noelle and her manager continue to disagree, not buying the merits of each other's position, Noelle feels her chest getting tighter and notices that she's breathing in shallow, quick breaths. Noelle realizes it's literally getting harder and harder to talk.

In this situation, Noelle can listen to her body, which is most likely transmitting, "You are feeling really worked up about something! This is probably an emergency!" She can also notice that as she clashes repeatedly with her manager, neither of them are really reaching the other. Because she notices these things and has some insight into what they mean, she may then be able to see that it's time to turn the conflict in a different direction. Or she could also call on other tactics to slow down, defuse, or exit the conflict altogether. In this way, her awareness of what her body and her gut are telling her helps her use other skills she's learned to constructively change the course of this conversation. (We'll learn about many of these skills in later chapters.)

Listening to your instincts isn't always the easiest way, mind you. "So often, good judgment comes from experience in which you exercised bad judgment. I really take that idea to heart," admits Rebecca Baker, chief marketing officer and global partner at Alvarez & Marsal. Allowing for some trial and error, including success and failure, can give you what you need to hone your own judgment.

Remember, little risk is involved in merely listening to your instincts; the leaps come when you take action. Although tuning in to your own thoughts on something, listening to your body, and deciding what to do with that information gives you more self-knowledge, it almost always equates to power. The chapters that follow will help you maneuver through situations, calling on all of these personal signals along with facts, context, and relationships. Your instinct, intuition, and self-knowledge will yield rich data throughout your life but only you decide how to use it.

MEET YOUR INNER RISK TAKER

There's a common experience that bonds women and can factor greatly into our propensity to push back. We can see pushback as a risk not worth taking, one that could sully, or worse, ruin our reputations. What's more, what might pushing back do to the relationship at hand? Many of us wonder, "Is my agenda really more important than keeping this connection intact?" We have the opportunity to take risks every day, whether fighting for the merit of an idea, changing jobs, or advocating on someone's behalf. We take risks when we ask for something that could be seen as an inconvenience or when we advocate to make almost any change.

In assessing her own propensity to take risks, Karen Ganzlin, chief human resources officer at TD Ameritrade, notes, "From a risk-taking perspective, I'm probably in the middle of the road. I'd never 'bet the farm,' even though lots of business success stories are based on people who do. I take a pretty calculated approach. One factor that makes us less likely to take risks is that we women are culturally sensitized and programmed not to take risks." Barbara J. Krumsiek, president, CEO, and chair of Calvert Investments, Inc., offers a similar perspective, saying, "I believe that women resist trial by error. That kind of avoidance of trying new things can be a career roadblock. You can't always know 100 percent of the information about something before you do it; it's okay to just know enough." The point is that although pushback will never be a pure, easily predictable science, and it often involves at least some risk, it doesn't need to be seen as dangerous by women.

And yet, peril and risk taking seem to be twin companions for many of us. "What I observe is that women are more cautious risk takers," remarks Susan McFarland. "Sometimes we're so concerned with being wrong that we hesitate more, whether it's entering a conversation or putting our position out there in a debate. We tend to be more hurt if we're challenged." No, risking doesn't come with promises and guarantees but you can guarantee yourself that your move is worth taking, whatever the outcome.

Having interviewed dozens of high-ranking leaders like Susan, I've learned they don't shy away from taking risks—instead they engage in activities considered to be "high risk" on a regular basis. "The lesson for women is: don't overestimate what others can do," advises Deborah Simpson. "Not too many people have 100 percent of the competencies for any role. There's lots of learning on the job that happens. Just ask yourself, 'Can I add value?' If so, then go for it." Similarly, Darlene Slaughter cites, "I heard at some point that I wasn't seen as enough of a risk taker. Don't be afraid to step outside your box. Take things you don't know how to do and propel yourself there anyway. Many times we say 'no' because we don't have 100 percent of the requirements. Seventy percent of the requirements is okay." These women executives see risk taking as a career necessity and link their high-stakes moves to their speedy career advancements. Operating with a resilient mind-set (rather than a perfectionist one), they have learned to identify which risks to take and to employ a variety of constructive approaches:

- They let go of the need for guaranteed outcomes. Common among women at the top is zero delusions that they can take on a risky project without actually assuming risk. They trust in the abilities they have grown over time to compensate for their weaker skills, knowing that a person with a perfectionist outlook won't execute risk well.
- They maintain a mind-set of resilience. Successful executives can't walk around believing, "This risk is going to ruin me," without it becoming a self-fulfilling prophecy. In fact, they see their own elasticity and ability to adapt to curveballs as a comfort. Their thick skin is helped by being optimistic, focusing on opportunities in favor of damages. They also tend to see failure as necessary for success.
- They enlist others in their success. Eric J. Mash, professor of psychology at the University of Calgary, found that the most resilient girls come from households that encourage risk taking and independence—balanced with support from an older female.[2] Similarly, women executives I've interviewed tend to be savvy enough to get knowledge and support from those more seasoned or expert than them. They "know what they don't know," which helps them strategically reach out to others and fill their gaps in knowledge.
- They operate, in a sense, as scientists. Established executives function in a space of learning, where mistakes—and measured failure—are expected. Much like a scientist who sets out with a hypothesis to prove or disprove, oftentimes the only way to validate an idea is to put it to the test. A scientist

learns from the process, incorporates that learning into her repertoire, and moves forward.

On Taking Risks

"I was very fortunate to grow up with parents who encouraged me to take risks. Through that reinforcement, I developed early in life a comfort level with going out on a limb knowing it could break. Risk taking has served me well throughout my career and, quite frankly, opened many doors that I would not otherwise have walked through over the years."

—Carol Ann Petren, executive vice president and general counsel, MacAndrews & Forbes Holdings Inc.

In order to go against the current, say the unpopular thing, or ask for something that no one's dreamed of asking for before—that is, in order to push back—you'll need a healthy tolerance for taking risks. "In truth, it's riskier *not* to put yourself out there," warns Susan McFarland. "You will simply not advance if you try to play it eternally safe."

Yes, a risk, like being the only one to advocate for approach A instead of approach B, will make your pulse quicken. It might make you seriously uncomfortable in your skin. But don't let the urge for likeability color your actions or stop you altogether. "Be fearless and take risks," advocates Lucy S. Danziger, editor-in-chief of *SELF Magazine*. "Growth doesn't always need to be incremental. Allow yourself to take big, bold steps in a new direction. And don't worry about the kinds of things that plague so many women: trying to please, being liked, and being successful all at the same time. Most successful people focus on following their gut and doing what feels right, rather than always trying to be liked." Risking and listening to your deepest nudges and urges are skills that take practice. It may very well make you sweat or cause your pulse to race. If that's the case, you know what you're doing probably involves pushback, your most flexible and needed skill set.

MAKE A PLAN AND MAKE A START

As with any change we hope to make, becoming our own best advocate and a discerning risk taker requires that we commit to a plan for long-term success. You can custom-build a system and plan for learning pushback skills by calling on the savvy you exercise every day to organize schedules, execute deliverables, and ensure high-quality work.

One effective approach is to create some dissonance—some disharmony—around the behavior you want to change. For example, you can begin attaching high discomfort and a negative association to your former way of doing things by reminding yourself, "When I don't ask, I end up resenting myself and everyone else" or "I hate the way I feel when I accept something, saying 'yes' when I really mean 'no.'" Psychologists will tell you that positively reinforcing your new behavior or preferred way of doing things is just as important. By dwelling on affirmatives and encouraging messages such as "I've never once regretted advocating my needs; I've almost always benefited as a result" or "I like the feeling of self-respect I have when I ask for what I really want," we can ignite a momentum in ourselves to keep the positive going.

Another method is to find the areas that feel important and difficult, and to run a series of low-stakes experiments trying out new skills and tactics for dealing with them. Your dreaded salary negotiation might be the first time you try out a pushback skill, but it doesn't have to be—try it in a restaurant, with your sister or with a colleague. Then notice, analyze, and even take notes on what happened and how it went. You can use the exercise that follows in this chapter as a format for picking your three most important power moves in any number of interactions. The principle here is that if you methodically practice a desired but difficult behavior, and reinforce it by analyzing it, it loses its emotional charge and begins to feel more natural and easier; it truly becomes a part of your makeup. Your confidence grows with the skill.

Think creatively about what system of learning and practice will work best for you. The important thing is that you make a commitment to learn new skills, set up a plan that will support your success, and make a start. Give yourself the freedom to experiment, fail, succeed, learn, and try again.

WON'T WE BE PUNISHED?

Inevitably, when I teach risk taking and pushback skills to my workshop participants, I hear at least one concerned woman remark, "Yes, but women will be penalized if they act too firmly or severely." To be fair, there is truth in such statements. When a woman assumes what psychologists call *agentic* behaviors, such as being confident and ambitious, men and women *both* feel less comfortable with her than if a man were displaying these same attributes.

Researchers at Rutgers University compared perceptions of men and women who interviewed for the same job. A male and female pair of actors was coached and instructed to display behaviors in a job interview associated with agentic qualities. The male and female actors were then taped while interviewing for a job. Study participants were asked to watch the tape and appraise the job applicants' competence, social skills, and hire-ability.

The women interviewees who presented themselves agentically were evaluated as competent but lacking social skills, which ultimately hurt their hire-ability. By contrast, confident and ambitious male candidates were evaluated as competent, likable, and were more likely to be hired than a woman with similar traits.[3]

Similarly, researchers at Catalyst, a research and advisory organization that looks to expand opportunities for women, did an equally eye-opening study about gender stereotypes. In it, senior-level executives were asked to independently rate the effectiveness of female and then male leaders on ten key leadership behaviors. Both men and women respondents cast women as better at stereotypically feminine "caretaking skills" such as rewarding and supporting. Yet both men and women asserted that men excel at more conventionally masculine "taking charge" skills such as influencing superiors and delegating responsibility. Interestingly these taking charge skills are what we use when we ask for what we want. Jeanine Prime, author of the study and director of research at Catalyst, notes, "It is often these 'taking charge' skills—the stereotypically 'masculine' behaviors—that are seen as prerequisites for top-level positions."[4]

No, this is not heartening data. It's already a challenge to tolerate conflict or seek out leadership. It can feel like climbing a very steep hill when other people undermine, underestimate, or undervalue you simply because you're a woman. Yet a change in how people perceive women will hinge on our making the change happen. As women, we need to claim what we want unapologetically and let men—and other women—get used to seeing us as powerful.

Society doesn't move forward because someone says, "Someone else can fight for it" or "Maybe the problem will fix itself." On the contrary, anything worth doing is rarely easy. My challenge to you, as the next generation of women leaders, is to choose to engage. Know what barriers are out there, acknowledge them, and then forge ahead anyway. You'll be helped if you can avoid the mind-set of, "The higher I fly, the farther I'll fall." DeeDee Wilson encourages, "No matter how much of a rock star you are at your job, you won't be a rock star all the time. That's okay. It just means you're challenging yourself." Practice fostering this kind of resiliency in yourself—the attitude that falling short always brings the gift of greater knowledge and valuable experience.

PUSHBACK AND YOU

Each of us will naturally excel at—and potentially struggle with—putting different pushback skills to the test. What equates to moving mountains for me might be something you can do in your sleep and vice versa. To help with this, the following assessment can help you pinpoint your particular areas of strength and become more aware of your weaker areas. There are no right or wrong answers but the more honest you are, the more actionable your results will be. Likewise, having weaknesses is no shame—we all have them. Knowing yours gives you power—and the opportunity to work on them!

Take a minute to reflect on your tendencies at work. Do you leverage your assertive qualities to create value for yourself and others? Review each of the following statements, putting an X next to the rating that most sounds like you.

	Rating Scale				
	Never Like Me	Seldom Like Me	About Half of the Time Like Me	Usually Like Me	Always Like Me
I dispute a situation if my needs aren't being met.					
When something doesn't work the first time, I keep trying to find ways to make it work.					
I speak up and ask if there's something I need.					
I have confidence in my ability to find solutions, no matter how big the problem.					
I'm good at thinking on my feet.					
I consider myself a creative, out-of-the-box thinker.					
I manage unanticipated problems with little difficulty.					
I believe it's better to voice problems and concerns than to hold them in.					
I am adept at noticing fluctuations in others' emotions.					
If I disagree with the popular point of view, I'm willing to challenge it.					
I am confident in my ability to recover from mistakes.					
I tolerate conflict well.					
I tend to focus on potential gains more than potential losses.					

Now look at where you have the ratings with the most agreement, under *usually like me* and *always like me*. Circle the two items that you think reflect your strongest skills. Next, look at the items you rated with the least agreement, under *never like me* and *seldom like me*. Circle the two items that you feel the least confident about.

Here's how each of these statements translates into a skill:

Skill Statement	What This Is Really About
I dispute a situation if my needs aren't being met.	Challenging status quo
When something doesn't work the first time, I keep trying to find ways to make it work.	Having grit and endurance
I speak up and ask if there's something I need.	Knowing my self-worth
I have confidence in my ability to find solutions, no matter how big the problem.	Creative problem solving
I'm good at thinking on my feet.	Extemporaneous thinking
I consider myself a creative, out-of-the-box thinker.	Generating alternatives
I manage unanticipated problems with little difficulty.	Having a resilient mind-set
I believe it's better to voice problems and concerns than to hold them in.	Confronting issues
I am adept at noticing fluctuations in others' emotions.	Using emotional intelligence
If I disagree with the popular point of view, I'm willing to challenge it.	Letting go of the need to conform
I am confident in my ability to recover from mistakes.	Avoiding perfectionist thinking
I tolerate conflict well.	Accepting disagreement
I tend to focus on potential gains more than potential losses.	Maintaining an optimistic outlook

As you think about your areas of strength, call to mind at least two occasions when each one has come powerfully into play for you. Doing so will help reinforce the realization that this skill is in fact a real strength (and not a one-time fluke). Let's say, for example, that I've identified that I'm good at "focusing on potential gains more than potential losses." I may recall the time I helped my teammates move past a major mistake on a project plan by salvaging the elements of the plan that were useable. I could also bring to mind the negotiation I was involved in with my boss, where I got two out of the four things I asked for and walked away satisfied with my net gains.

Then, for your three weakest areas, reflect on what specifically is difficult about each, noting how you might work on it. For example, if "I'm good at thinking on my feet" is a skill I struggle with, it would help to know that pressure, without preparation, tends to make me anxious, which does the opposite of helping me think creatively. One thing I could do to combat this kind of anxious cycle is to get more comfortable with pressure and extemporaneous thinking. Perhaps an improvisation class could allow me to have fun and practice in a low-stakes environment.

Finish your personal growth strategy by considering that everyone has a whole spectrum of strengths and weaknesses—and it is a true strength to know where yours lie. This exercise, like many elements of this book, is a lesson in self-knowledge and one that I encourage you to come back and revisit in six months or a year. You'll be able to reflect on movement in your weaknesses as well as the solidifying of your strengths. Remember, know yourself before you attempt to know anyone or anything else in a pushback situation.

Your Personal Pushback Style

As you continue building and fine-tuning your pushback skills, consider your reputation. How are you known? Now call to mind a clear picture of how you ideally want to behave in the world, how you want to be perceived, and what you'd like to stand for. Do the two match—your current reputation and your ideal one? Where they do not match, and especially where they actively conflict, you have room for growth—and a goal to grow toward. Be strategic about the reputation and skills you want to embody—by looking into the future—and you can actively sculpt your image rather than letting it happen to you. "The most important thing you have is your reputation," says Darlene Slaughter. "When you show up at the door, people will already have an opinion of you. They'll wonder, Can she get the job done? Can she deal with people? How does she manage the tough times? What about the good times? What kind of character does she have? All these things go into promoting someone to the next level."

Darlene's points get to the heart of the importance of having your own vision or credo for how you'll demonstrate your power—how you'll push back. The next exercise yields an expression of your credo that can serve in tough conversations to anchor you and remind you of your personal modus operandi. In using it, you can preserve your own authenticity in challenging situations, checking your current approach against your credo, seeing if your behaviors are where you want them to be.

Do You See Pushback as a Challenge or a Threat?

Albert Bandura, a Stanford professor and expert on self-efficacy, or the belief in one's own abilities, has much to teach us about pushing back. Bandura's research shows that those with high self-efficacy see tough, meaty tasks as provocative challenges rather than damage-imposing threats. When things don't go as these people hope, those with high self-efficacy tend to be understanding, tenacious in not giving up, and have even been known to have a sense of humor about their errors.[5]

Your Pushback Credo

Write out two qualities that are most important to you to portray in a conflict, negotiation, or tough conversation, such as *fair-minded, firm, flexible, empathetic, strong, calm,* or *decisive.*

_____   _____

A   B

Write out two actions that are most important to you to embody in a negotiation, such as *inviting other viewpoints, coming up with creative options, keeping an optimistic mind-set, surfacing problems honestly,* or *treating counterparts as equals.*

_____   _____

C   D

Now put it all together.

"No matter how heated the debate, I take an approach that allows me to be _____ A _____ and _____ B _____. By _____ C _____ and _____ D _____, I do everything possible to find mutually beneficial solutions, separating the person from the problem at hand. I don't back down easily; I'm respectful of the person but hard on the problem."

You can equip yourself for any situation when you're grounded in who you are. By reviewing your credo before and even during a tough conversation, you can give yourself a touchstone based on your long-term vision and your values—something many of us need when our blood is boiling, a conversation is getting tense, or anticipation is overwhelming us. Rather than just thinking about right now, this minute, we can expand our point of view, seeing things more broadly. Along with your credo, you can ask yourself, as a reality check, "Is how I'm behaving in line with the kind of brand I want to embody or the legacy I want to leave? If not, how can I retool my approach?" Such touchstones give you the ultimate compass for important decisions and maneuvers, and a clear picture of your values.

If you're going to push back masterfully and enjoy the sense of accomplishment that comes with it, it'll help to believe that you have all the ingredients needed—right now—to take on the world. Carol Dweck, a social and developmental psychologist at Stanford University, has shed some critically important light on this area. Since graduate school, Dweck has been interested in how students cope with difficulty, for example, why in one case difficulty turned out to be a terrible indictment and in another case difficulty represented an exciting challenge:

> In one of my very first studies where I was giving failure problems, this little boy rubbed his hands together, smacked his lips, and said, "I love a challenge." And I thought, "Where is this kid from? Is he from another planet?" Either you cope with failure or you don't cope with failure, but to love it? That was something that was beyond my understanding, and I thought, "I'm going to figure out what this kid knows, and I'm going to bottle it." Over time I came to understand a framework in which you could relish something that someone else was considering a failure.[6]

Dweck's research on what motivates us supports the idea that a *growth mind-set,* as she puts it, or seeing intelligence as a changeable, fluid characteristic that can be developed with effort, leads to greater persistence when faced with adversity. This is opposed to a *fixed mind-set,* in which we view intelligence as an innate, uncontrollable attribute.[7] Disqualifying ourselves with statements such as, "I don't do conflict" or "I'm not a negotiator" undermines the fact that these skills are completely learnable ones that we can master over time—or may already possess.

Dweck's findings also show that those with a fixed mind-set tend to lose confidence when they encounter challenges because they believe that if they are truly "smart," things will come easily to them. If they must persevere, they question their abilities and lose belief in themselves, tending to give up because they deem they are "not good" at the task and, because their intelligence is fixed, will never be good at it.

By contrast, those with a growth mind-set tend to believe in the power of effort. In the face of difficulty, their confidence actually grows because they believe they are learning and getting smarter as a result of challenging themselves. Dweck and her colleagues found that students—in middle school and college—are about equally divided between the two mind-sets.

Which camp are you in? Are you one to see difficulty or complex issues with dread or do you grab on to such experiences knowing that somehow you'll rise to the challenge? Do you think you've been given a hand that you're stuck with or do you see your own potential as limitless? If you're going to persevere, it pays to boost your levels of resilience and grit. These magic qualities, which can certainly be grown, come in handy when we're confronted by opposition. Here are a few questions that will help you come to a personal under-standing of grit, resilience, and persistence. The first two questions explore what grit looks like—in someone you know and in yourself. The second two questions can be used when you are facing a tough situation—to remind you that you can find the resources (internal and external) and the stick-to-it-iveness to get through any challenge.

- Think of someone you admire for their gutsiness or persis-tence. What makes them different from others? Think of a time when they really showed their grit. What did that look like?
- When have I surpassed my own idea of what I could do? What conditions helped me take that risk?
- What would it take for me to be *comfortable enough* to do this? Is there a person, resource, or service that could boost my skills or confidence?
- How could I break this down or make it more manageable, taking a baby step toward what I want?

Although it's hard to get in touch with your grit when you're simply going along through life, you'll no doubt realize what you're made of when faced with something that makes you squirm. Rebecca Baker talks about this when she says, "There's an evolution in your career. When you go from managing to leading, for example, there's a monumental risk involved. You subject yourself to a ton of pushback. The key is your attitude and instinct. . . . " Following the advice in this book—facing your strengths and weaknesses, seeking out learning experiences, leading an initiative, building up and testing your tolerance for risk—can open windows into a new world, giving you opportunities to refine your skills, broaden you as a person, and build your confidence. Or pushback skills can remain uncomfortable and unpleasant, like going to the dentist. You can decide which.

Go Get It!

In 2010, Sheryl Sandberg, chief operating officer of Facebook, delivered a fifteen-minute speech that created quite a media storm at a conference sponsored by TED, a nonprofit dedicated to sharing "ideas worth spreading." Sandberg's speech focused on women and leadership and produced the most shared, e-mailed, and discussed talk I've witnessed in the leadership arena. Just what was it that compelled people to pass this video clip on and on? The reason Sandberg's message resonated so much is that she urged women to "go get it" rather than waiting for permission.[8]

Sandberg summoned women to keep their foot on the gas pedal of their careers, even if they may want to off-ramp in the future. She reasoned that since the beginning of time, men have overestimated their abilities—and women have underestimated theirs. She gave a sense to the women in that room (and the thousands of others who later shared in the experience) that we have a substantive hand in creating our own future.

No matter what pushback situation you find yourself in, the greater impact is often larger than what you see. What you advocate for right now will have an effect on your future. And when you push for a change that could positively affect you, it very well may also yield a positive impact for others.

When I asked Sheila Murphy what piece of advice stayed with her most over the years, she recalled a vivid story. "Someone once told me that when she got promoted she received a letter from another female executive. It said, '*Behind every woman who gets promoted is herself.*' You have to sell your work, your projects, and put the time in to expand your reputation. You can't do good work and expect to just get noticed." Sheila emphasizes that results *plus our own willingness to advocate* are job requirements for those who want to move up. Engaging in pushback when you don't like the status quo will open up a world of options for you. Now, let's get ready to go a few rounds.

The next four chapters lay out the four steps of my system for negotiating and advocacy. As mentioned previously, I favor a consultative style of negotiating that I feel complements women's strengths—and is extremely effective. Chapters Three and Four deal with preparation, Chapter Five gives you tactics and strategies for the conversation itself, and Chapter Six is about following up—the crucial final stage of any well-handled negotiation. In Chapter Three, you'll continue the work of self-exploration you started in this chapter, sussing out your strengths, weaknesses, and style preferences when it comes to negotiation.

3

Prepare Psychologically

Atimeless story involves a woman who's getting ready for the hardest negotiation of her career. She owns a company that is likely to be acquired and the only way she'll go through with the acquisition is if the bulk of her workforce can keep their jobs. The acquiring company is pushing back on that request.

Just prior to the negotiation, she steps into a room nearby to go over her notes one last time. As she paces back and forth, scanning her notes and gesturing emphatically, a man comes in and asks her what she's doing. Surprised, she says, "I'm preparing for an important meeting—a negotiation—that starts in a few minutes."

The man said, "Very interesting. Tell me, do you ever get nervous before a negotiation?"

"Of course not," the woman said.

"Well," he said, "would you tell me what you're doing in the men's room?"

Many of us ignore the emotions of negotiating, thinking that "more information" is the key to success. Surely one more statistic, figure, or piece of rationale will give us the edge we need to get what we want (these things matter, of course, and we'll talk about them in the next chapter). Yet, emotions are the very forces that can drive negotiations to break down, escalate to unmanageable levels, or not even happen in the first place. In fact, when two parties discount the role of emotion in the conversation, they can carry on in a surface-level dance that focuses—mistakenly—on demands and positions rather than deeper interests.

Although having a strong factual case is critical, emotional and psychological preparation is equally as important. You need not wing it every time you have a negotiation; rather, you can deliberately harness your natural power by consistently identifying your emotions and incorporating them strategically in conversations. As unlikely as it may seem, emotions can serve not as roadblocks but as an engine propelling your case forward. Understanding and working with your own emotions—and being savvy about those of your counterpart—will give you data you can use to your best advantage.

Learning to prepare psychologically has a number of disparate facets—in fact, more than you might expect. From overcoming the deep-seated good-girlisms that many of us have been schooled in, to calming pregame jitters, you'll find in this chapter that bending to and channeling your emotions rather than merely controlling them ups your power and confidence. You will learn how to strategically use empathy to extract your counterpart's deeper needs and see how preparation, done the right way, can quell your anxiety. Perhaps most important, you'll find that the psychological stamina needed to manage and navigate pushback will cascade into other parts of your life, arming you with confidence and a greater sense of your own voice.

WHO DO YOU THINK YOU ARE?

One of the greatest negotiating tools at your disposal is a clear understanding of yourself. Rebecca Baker, chief marketing officer and global partner, Alvarez & Marsal, talked about this skill, noting, "I've always been pretty clear on my talents, abilities, and the best environments for me. I've always been a go-getter. In my twenties and thirties, I turned what I didn't know into a strength. I did not self-impose limitations or over-think things. Nothing really stopped me from acting and taking initiative." Your psychological style may differ from Rebecca's; the point is that whatever it is, understanding it lets you leverage its strengths.

Self-command—made up of self-knowledge plus self-management skills—is a supremely underestimated asset for becoming an expert at pushback. Whether by working through the exercises in this book or through other means, make it your business to know what and who you're bringing to the negotiation table.

You can build on your self-knowledge by taking personality inventories such as the Myers-Briggs Type Indicator and The Mayer-Salovey-Caruso Emotional Intelligence Test and looking for the patterns in what they're telling you about yourself. Even better, ask a handful of people you trust to share with you two of your gifts—those areas where you really shine—and two ways that you tend to hold yourself back. You will be amazed by the helpful, eye-opening, and often validating feedback you'll get.

While on my own self-exploratory mission a few years ago, I can remember paying an expensive executive coach to give me feedback on my presentation abilities. At the time, I was doing fifty presentations a year and with a different audience each time. I wondered if I was really improving as a presenter or if I was chugging along in a vacuum, missing important insights. Although the coach ultimately gave me helpful feedback, nothing could substitute for the powerful learning I got from seeing myself presenting on camera. In watching myself on film, I noticed that in my zeal to be professional and not—horror of horrors—come across as too young, I was stiffening my body and deadening my emotions at various points in my speech. Given my huge enthusiasm for my topic, "no emotion" was the last message I ever wanted to convey. This video feedback has been invaluable in helping to bring more of my natural passion to my speaking. This story also illustrates that *how* you learn about your strengths and weaknesses is not nearly as important as *that* you learn. Be creative in where and how you solicit input.

Perhaps one of the best self-branding techniques is to beat people to the punch with regard to feedback. Rather than waiting for them to inform you of your performance, ask, "Greg, you just saw me present in there. Tell me one thing I did well and one thing I should try to do better next time." Not only will you begin to see a blueprint of your own needs for improvement, you'll get an incredible handle on your signature strengths.

Rosemary Turner, president of Chesapeake UPS, suggests, "I ask myself often, 'Did I achieve what I wanted? Did that one-on-one with the CEO of the company go the way I envisioned it?' Sometimes the answer is no. Sometimes I think, 'I shouldn't have worn that jacket or explained my idea that way. I wasn't being totally me.' Self-reflection, I've found, has played a dramatic role in me moving up. I'm always asking myself if there's something I could've done differently." Taking ownership and having a voice will always be an easier task when you know who you are. Other pushback skills improve with self-knowledge, too—your decision-making abilities and understanding of your own personal values, in the short and long term, will get much better.

Make self-knowledge a mind-set. Ever deeper knowledge of yourself—what makes you tick and how you come across to others—can and should be a tool of continual self-improvement. And self-knowledge springs from experience. Let yourself try things, even if they're new or seem difficult. Set yourself up for successes, analyze failures, think about the techniques you used and about how you felt preparing for and going into the situation. How did it go? How did you feel? All this information, satisfying and uncomfortable alike, is potentially useful. And it's just information, not a judgment on you as a person or a professional. Ask yourself, Is this fixed or open thinking? Did that feel like a trip to the dentist or a wrestling match? Am I being hampered by perfectionistic thinking, fear of conflict, or a secret hope that I'll get what I want and need without having to demand it?

Approach experience and the self-knowledge it brings with curiosity and anticipation, not with perfectionism or disappointment that your strengths are *these* and not *those,* or that your weaknesses are areas you wish were strengths. Strengths are power you already have and they can be leveraged in many situations. Weaknesses are even better—they're opportunities for growth and learning.

Your Negotiating Roots

Before you set the world on fire with your negotiating talent, let's first look at where you've come from. In assessing her own conditioning, Deborah Simpson, chief financial officer of The Boston Consulting Group, noted, " . . . I'm not shy and I don't have a problem with being challenged. Having grown up with sisters, I think there was less built-in expectation that I'd take a seat at the table and simply let others do the talking." What about you? Considering some of your earliest life experiences, take a few minutes to work through the exercise My Negotiating Roots.

In my own personal development as a negotiator, a major revelation was uncovering that I had always thought I should be a "good girl." I wish I could say that I felt this only as a kid but I was burdened with this expectation into adulthood, a fact that cut most of my negotiations off at the knees. In my playbook, being a good girl meant being agreeable, nice, modest, accommodating, and easygoing. It did not mean speaking out, asking for something, or arguing a point, however important. After all, how could a good girl be powerful *and* nice?

My Negotiating Roots

- What did your family teach you about negotiating? Was advocating on one's own behalf off-limits, repressed, welcome, used little or often?
- What negotiating approach did those around you favor most? Were they aggressive, cooperative, indirect, passive, or constructive? Did they not negotiate?
- Do early memories bring up negative or positive emotions about negotiating?
- When you were a child, was it acceptable for girls to push back?
- How did you get what you wanted as a child?
- What other major experiences or factors have shaped you as a negotiator (or as someone who avoids negotiating)?

This discovery was key in helping me come up with a new paradigm for how I wanted to approach asking for what I wanted. As a young management consultant in my twenties, I started to grow tired of tiptoeing through my own life. If I had an idea in a meeting, I qualified it three different ways before offering it up (think, "This may be a silly idea but..." or "I might be wrong here..."). I saw it in my personal life, too. If it was time to choose a restaurant, I let others take charge and chimed in last so as not to be too outspoken.

Slowly, I started learning to be more direct. I worried less about being sweet and more about what I really wanted, along with the soundness of my argument. Then a funny thing happened. The more I took risks and started to say what I really thought or ask for what I really wanted, the more I earned a reputation for not just candor, but also results. Looking back at my old way of doing things, I can see that I was so busy trying to couch something in just the right way to make it palatable that the thrust of my message got diluted and my input had less impact than it could have had.

I held myself back due to some of my early programming and I saw my friends doing the same. I suspect that in some way, the same may be true for you. The more you can understand what your past encoding is about negotiating, the more power you have in sculpting a new identity. Rosemary Turner talks about this concept, noting, "I worried so much early on in my career. I worried about what I was wearing, what I said, and how I delivered it. I felt that I needed to put a face on at work and be someone different. At one point, I got tired of trying to be someone else and decided to bring my entire self to the job. What I found was that my performance went up right away." When you think about it that way, perhaps being a good girl isn't our destiny. Bringing our whole selves to work is better for everyone.

THE LOCUS OF CONTROL

Although looking back at what we learned from our family is essential, so is examining the messages we've absorbed from society at large. The princess stories of our youth involving elaborate ordeals, women in need of rescuing, and valiant acts on the part of men are partly to blame for discouraging women from advocating for their needs. Consider the commonalities in tales such as Cinderella, Rapunzel, and Snow White. You'll find that all of these stories depict women facing dire straits from which they can't save themselves. These women are relatively meek, even in the face of their desire to change their circumstances. Men dash in—rescuing these women from harm—which is the key to the women's lives moving happily forward. Social psychologists explain this concept as the *locus of control*, or the extent to which we believe we can affect the forces around us. Girls are largely reared to believe that their locus of control sits outside of them and that someone else will save them. Boys are typically taught that their locus of control resides within them, that they are the masters of their own destiny.

What's more, researchers have shown that the locus of control is the personality characteristic that provides the most consistent and the strongest evidence of how we moderate stress. The more outer our locus of control is, the more stress we tend to experience. Still, when surveyed, women tend to believe that they have less control over interpersonal relationships and uncontrollable life events than men have. Taken together, it's not surprising that researchers in the areas of stress have indicated repeatedly the beneficial effect of internal-control beliefs on well-being.[1]

With conditioning like this, is it any wonder we women sometimes find ourselves waiting to be saved? When we teach girls to believe that outer forces will help them, we minimize their self-agency. Certainly the concept of "someday your prince will come" leaches our power rather than helping us own it. As it is, some of the traits that are most important for us to demonstrate as credible adult leaders are deemphasized in girlhood. Indeed, many an executive I've interviewed has explained the significant pressure she has experienced from many sets of eyes watching her performance (and some waiting for her to fall)—underscoring how strong a woman leader must be. And yet, *strong* is not the first thing many of us were taught to associate with ourselves as girls.

GOOD GIRLS DON'T ASK

Beyond your conditioning, uncovering your attitude toward a bargaining situation drives the outcome more than you might think. Linda Babcock and Sara Laschever did some truly invaluable research on gender and negotiations, which culminated in their landmark book, *Women Don't Ask: Negotiation and the Gender Divide*. In one of their eye-opening studies, Babcock and Laschever found that women have a less optimistic view of the possible outcomes of their negotiations, creating a dynamic in which they ask for less—on average, 30 percent less—than men do.[2] One's outlook and attitude about negotiating can color the entire "ask," often halting it before it's even started. Does any of this resonate with your own experiences? If so, use the following exercise to go beyond surface information and look for deeper insight into your negotiation tendencies. Our best negotiation lessons often come in the form of successes but our regrets also have a lot to teach.

Try to remember three times you avoided negotiating for something and write them down. Next to each, write down the root cause for not moving forward. Use another sheet of paper to write more about either the ask you avoided or the root cause of your avoidance. For example:

> I didn't ask for better terms concerning my maternity leave plan. The root cause of my avoidance had to do with a fear of looking entitled and "full of myself." After all, why do I deserve special treatment?

I didn't negotiate for: Root cause(s) of my avoidance:

1. _____   _____

2. _____   _____

3. _____   _____

Now circle the situation that you most regret not pursuing. You can call to mind past regrets next time you need to ask for something, knowing that regrets can be as motivating as successes.

THE RELATIONSHIP TRAP

One particular message that is pushed on young women has particularly disastrous effects when it comes to the negotiations we engage in as adults. Girls are taught to accommodate others—to ease discomfort and service others' needs—a skill quite different, in fact opposite, from asking others for accommodations. As mentioned in Chapter One, a significant reason that women underposition themselves is a desire to preserve relationships. We can put such a significant focus on forming and maintaining relationships—and it's a trait that helps us in many ways in business but can handicap us in negotiations.

Certainly, relationships are critical in the workplace. Story after story illustrates that many a promotion has been achieved through knowing the right people and having good relationships with them. In fact, Alex Pentland, director of MIT's Human Dynamics Laboratory and the MIT Media Lab Entrepreneurship Program, has even shown that those with strong relationships tend to be more productive, by a large margin, than those who don't bother to network.[3] Although that may be the case, each of us needs to leave room for conflict or lack of agreement at work, knowing and expecting that there will be instances when we need to push back. We'll need to carefully weigh when the relationship is more important than the outcome for which we are advocating, and also realistically assess whether it's truly an either-or situation—the relationship or the outcome. It very rarely is. Ask yourself the following questions:

- What's the history of my relationship with this person? How does that color this conversation?
- What's the worst that can happen to the relationship as a result of having this conversation? if the conversation get contentious? if I'm overruled?
- How does the importance of my need stack up against maintaining friendly relations with this person? How fragile is the relationship at hand?

- Where do I stand on the issue? Where do I stand with the person? How can I keep the two separate?

Above all, we can understand that negotiation is not opposed to relationship, but utterly integral to it.

How Do You Do Conflict?

These questions begin to illustrate that there are numerous ways that you can approach pushback situations. We may lead with our power and authority in one situation and a team-centric, rapport-building approach in another. We may choose to skip negotiating altogether given certain constraints or we may take a more transactional, one-time approach based on the situation at hand. Each of these styles has merit and, ideally, we can learn to call on whichever serves the situation at hand.

If you disagree with your company's changes to the benefit plan and have already voiced your dissatisfaction twice regarding the new medical and dental insurance, you may pick your battles and not push back at all when you're displeased with changes to the 401K plan. Your decision will be influenced by your company's culture, your understanding of why the policy shifts are being made, and the personalities and relationships involved. You'll also consider your own reputation and desire not to beat your head against a wall and to save your ammunition for a fight that matters more or that you have a better shot at winning.

In a case where you're in charge, you may need to be clear with people that although you're soliciting their opinions, you have ultimate say and veto power. "As the chair of my firm's Finance committee—a committee that reports directly to our management on the finances of the firm—I've learned some things about handling pushback," recalls Catherine Ann Mohan, partner and treasurer at McCarter & English. "One thing that's helped me in this role is to listen to others' views but to be clear that I will make the final decision."

In a different setting—when there's an oppositional feeling in the room, when the final decision isn't yours, or when the power dynamics are not entirely clear—you might favor a collaborative approach, treating problems as "we versus the problem" not "you versus me."

In yet another situation—and you may be surprised to see me advocate for this—our best technique will be to take an avoidance approach. Take a dealing with a client or customer. In a world in which the customer is always right, good customer service representatives resolve issues by minimizing disagreement and fixing the problem at all costs. Avoiding conflict in favor of restoring harmony to a situation may indeed be the way to go sometimes. Note that minimizing conflict, whether with a client, colleague, or boss, done strategically and with a clear rationale in mind, is not the same as being afraid to negotiate and therefore being too paralyzed to take action. Always strive to tell yourself the truth about why you're choosing one path over another.

It's important to be aware of where you gravitate when faced with a negotiation. Do you capitulate too quickly? Stand your ground effectively? See only one way to win and succeed? Whatever your dominant style, know that you will learn more and get further by trying styles on than by sidestepping negotiation altogether. After all, although your own self-respect may be harmed by not negotiating, chances are good that your image will be hurt, too. Kathleen L. McGinn, professor at Harvard Business School, comments on this effect using compensation as an example. "Concerning salary negotiations, we hear women say, 'I don't want people to think

I'm too aggressive.' But if you flip that around, the perception of you when you don't negotiate is much more negative than the perception of you when you do negotiate. So in wanting everyone to look positively on our behavior—which is a stereotype—one of the things we can do is ask, 'How am I really going to be perceived if I don't negotiate?' If you don't negotiate for your salary, they walk away happy that they paid you less but wonder why they hired you."[4]

THE EFFECT OF FACT FINDING ON EMOTION

Many of us underestimate how much being prepared informationally can help us emotionally. Making a good case for your request means arming yourself with as much supporting evidence, research, and information as possible (something we will cover in depth in Chapter Four). Often data and evidence translate to leverage in a negotiation, and leverage increases your bank account of negotiation bargaining chips.

Walking into a negotiation without having done preparation or review of the issue at hand can be disastrous for your performance, as can a spontaneous or emotion-driven approach. The better prepared you are in terms of the facts, the more able you are to keep a calm and controlled demeanor and the more successful you are likely to be. Writing out the reasons you are negotiating is just a starting point, if an important one. Once you're clear on why you're advocating for a particular matter and you begin to assemble any supporting research, you'll notice that the more relevant research you have, the more compelling your case will be and the better you will feel about it. The better your case and the stronger your confidence in it, the more likely you are to push back, be creative, and find a solution that satisfies you. Similarly, when we understand the perspective of the individuals we'll be negotiating with in advance of the negotiation, we can tailor our message to fit their current demands and goals, upping our chances of being successful.

So, if for example you were going to ask for an assistant, you would do research within your company to see what the standard criteria are for hiring an assistant. Being able to answer, "How many people does an assistant typically support? How senior does one have to be to have an assistant? What kind of revenue does a department have to produce in order to justify having an assistant?" and other such questions not only bolsters your case but serves as a foundation for your emotional stability. You also want to look at the constraints and the needs of the person you will be negotiating with, preferably showing how he or she will benefit, too, with fulfilling your request.

What Do You Want and Why?

Before you begin building a case for the other person, ask yourself why you're requesting something in the first place. Uncover the difference between your position on a matter (for example, "I'd rather not take on that client assignment in Zurich") versus your deeper concerns and interests (for example, "I'm afraid if I say yes to this request, travel demands on me will become unmanageable" or "I'm committed to the firm, but I'm uncomfortable being that far away from my young children for four nights").

These deeper, underlying reasons for our argument are a key factor in getting win-win outcomes. After all, a true negotiation relies on *inter*dependence. We need to convince and work with the other side to get what we want. This is also the chief reason that steamrolling or a dictatorial style doesn't work in negotiations. You can use the following examples to help tease apart why you're sitting at the negotiation table in the first place.

Position (What)	Interest (Why)
I'd like your blessing to apply for the marketing associate role in the next department.	I'm no longer engaged in my role. I don't like finance as much as I thought I would.
I'm proposing I move to a compressed, four-day work week.	I'd like some say over how my work gets done. I'd like more flexibility in my schedule.
I'd like a 10 percent pay raise.	I'd like recognition of my performance and contributions. I'd like to know my compensation is on par with other top performers.
I'd like to be made project manager of the new client account.	I'm no longer challenged in my role. I'm hungry to grow my skills and learn something new.

Although you should be prepared to think through your own positions versus interests, you should also feel comfortable identifying and clarifying your counterparts' motives, something you will learn about in Chapter Four. For now, remember that when it comes to your own position, the simplest way to get to the heart of the matter is to ask a question that resembles, "Why?" You can and should ask yourself, "Why do I see ABC as the only answer to the problem?" or "How did I arrive at that conclusion?"

I spoke to Susan McFarland, executive vice president and principal accounting officer at Capital One, about understanding why we're really sitting at the negotiation table. "Early in my career, I did lots of what didn't work well in trying to make a case for something. . . . Figure out what you really want and what you're willing to accept. Often we don't think that through before the discussion. Then, we settle for something outside our hoped-for range." Your own self-knowledge is the most important foundation on which you'll build a case.

As you prepare for any negotiation, ready yourself by thinking through the following questions:

- What am I asking for? What is my position?
- What do I really want? What are my interests?
- Is there only one way to get what I truly want? If not, what are my other options?

KNOW YOUR POWER

Having your own emotions in good order is crucial (as is having a well-built case). But your standing or leverage with another person may have an even stronger influence on your success. No matter what the situation, negotiation always boils down to a predictable dance around the thing a person has that her counterpoint wants. Before any negotiation, ask yourself where and how you have leverage. Whether your leverage is your experience, tenure, skills, book of business or client base, education, or a combination of these factors, you can't convey confidence without knowing your power.

Women in particular may avoid using their leverage or self-promoting because they worry that they will look arrogant, overbearing, or foolish. Peggy Klaus, an expert on self-promotion and author of *Brag! The Art of Tooting Your Own Horn Without Blowing It*, reminds us that a job well done does not speak for itself, nor does humility get you noticed. Klaus notes that women may be programmed to think "good girls don't brag,"[5] stopping them from leveraging their accomplishments to get more of what they want.

One technique that will help you surmount any fears you have about bragging is simply this: keep your self-promotion fact based. For example, if you brought in $20,000 in repeat business, ten new client projects, or saved the company 3 percent of operating costs, share those facts and stand behind them. It will be much harder for the other side to refute or find fault with your case and, to repeat a mantra I use every single time I present to a group of women, "If it's true, it's not bragging."

If it helps, here's another perspective on the value of self-promotion. "Self advocacy hasn't always come naturally to me," says Irene Chang Britt, chief strategy officer at Campbell Soup Company. "I'm Asian, so there's an expectation I should be deferential and not toot my own horn. The advice that's helped me improve most is to speak about achievements as best practices, as learning for the greater good. It's also important to share team accomplishments, to advocate for others, and let other people be the heroes." The art of pushing back will require you to claim and promote your needs, accomplishments, and value. Find a voice for conveying these contributions and advocating for your needs and your agenda will be far simpler.

FIND INVISIBLE GUIDES

As you get ready emotionally, don't forget the power of your peers. One of my favorite career discoveries has been finding role models who can help me, yet who may never even know they taught me. I'm talking about people I've watched handle pushback situations skillfully, using observation to see how they navigate debates and regulate their emotions. We are surrounded every day by talent, so why not tap into it? Sheila Murphy, associate general counsel at MetLife, notes, "You'll get better at negotiating by doing it and observing others. I've learned more from observing my skilled counterparts, often after the fact, than I have from my own performance. When you negotiate with someone who's good, ask yourself, 'What are they doing? Is it successful? Can I incorporate it into my bag of tricks?'" Surely you can watch others for technical cues but dealing with emotions may require you to talk to them.

You might later ask someone you observed, "How did you manage to take that 'no' so well? How did you get him to ultimately say 'yes,' not letting the initial rejection lower your expectations or lower your performance?"

To be sure, engaged mentors and guides can also give you critical information and suggest angles that you may not have thought of. "Get mentors early and for different things. Mentors can really accelerate your advancement," encourages Rebecca Baker. Guides and teachers, which is essentially what mentors are, can also buoy our confidence and courage, two necessities for negotiating.

ATTITUDE'S ROLE IN APTITUDE

As you ready yourself to negotiate, take the time to find your ideal outlook. You can strive for a composed balance somewhere between energized and relaxed. You want to convey not only that "I'm okay, you're okay," but also that you can be firm about an issue and yet respectful of the person.

You also want to focus on engaging in balanced thinking if you're someone who tends to see doom and gloom arising in a negotiation. Balanced thinking means that if we see the potential downside to a situation, we must, as a matter of habit, imagine the upside of the event. In other words, if you're going to face your fears, then you also have to face what could go right! Insisting on balanced thinking can steer us away from pessimism and low confidence. What's more, you'll find that this habit becomes increasingly easy to develop.

Lori A. Greenawalt, partner at KPMG LLP, illustrates this point exactly. "I was sought out by a different company and given an attractive offer. The company had been my client, there were stock options involved, and they were going public in a few months.

I debated that offer back and forth for a while. I asked, 'What's the best thing that could happen? What would it be like if it went famously well?' I always consider, 'If the best thing happens in this situation, where am I and how would I feel?' Then I play the inverse: 'What if someone else takes the new job (and risk) and the best thing happens to them? How would I feel about that?' I let this sit for a period of time and I can usually come up with an answer that feels right." Balanced thinking can restore rationality to your analysis or help you size up a situation.

Still, preparing for a confrontation or negotiation can invoke discomfort and fear. Yet, by not allowing yourself to wallow or get stuck in "analysis paralysis," you might feel temporary discomfort and yet move forward, unencumbered. Remember, getting stuck in overanalysis and rehearsing feelings of fear are a choice; you don't have to engage in them.

Are You Entitled?

Social psychologist Brenda Major studied gender differences in entitlement, or what people think they deserve. Students were told to indicate what they should be paid for a fixed amount of work. Repeatedly, the studies showed that men noted they should be paid more money than did women.[6]

Given that negotiation conversations can feel confrontational to many women, it's critical to fill yourself with positive, empowering messages in advance of the negotiation. Above all, decide that you're entitled; you have a place at the negotiation table and a right to ask for what you want. If you're afraid, remind yourself of what prompted you to go after more in the first place. Don't be fearful of reaching high just because women have been known to typically set lower targets than men.

Carefully separate for yourself the person you will be speaking with and the problem you are trying to solve—they are not the same. Your attitude—whether good, bad, or indifferent—will leak out no matter how hard you to try to conceal it, so make sure that you've worked to get yourself in a confident, positive mental space.

Boost yourself up emotionally by dwelling on your strength and abilities. Concentrate on several of your past successes to increase your confidence and optimism. "Do things with good intent, a higher purpose, and show the collective advantage. . . . It's helped my confidence to walk into a meeting with a certain gravitas from past successes," says Rebecca Baker. You too can buttress your preparation by focusing on your signature strengths. The following questions can guide you:

- Is there something or someone who can boost my confidence in this area?
- Is there someone who's done something similar to what I want to do?
- Are there success stories on this subject?
- Is there an existing group or community of practice that knows about this?
- Is there a way I can pivot my learning from one area of my life to another to accomplish this?
- Is there someone who can hold me accountable and support me?
- What is the worst that could happen if I go for it?
- What if the outcome of this is a smash success?
- What will *not* happen for me if I don't take this risk? Is that okay with me?

If you can answer these questions for yourself, you can more easily exude a positive and approachable attitude going into a negotiation, which means that you're more likely to convey that you are interested in both parties gaining from the discussion. Key into your motivations and foresee a favorable result. This will help to put the person you are negotiating with at ease from the beginning.

ROLE-PLAY

Invite two trusted friends, partners, classmates, mentors, or colleagues to role-play an upcoming negotiation with you. Ask one person to play your negotiation counterpart. You may want to ask the pretend counterpart to be fair and balanced the first time, and then to role-play a second or third time in a tougher manner, expressing more criticism of the request or providing more pushback.

On Getting Centered

"Mentally, I do lots of scenario testing. I carefully try to anticipate objections. What if they counter? What if they tear my argument apart?

... If I'm anticipating a really tough conversation, I usually give myself time beforehand to pause. I ask myself, 'What will it take for me to remain focused in there?' If I can avoid scheduling a meeting or event right before a negotiation I will so that I have time to center myself. I do not want to let my emotions go every which way.

I've been known to take a week off work before a major deal. Once I did this at a spa in Colorado, where I really relaxed and meditated. I got comfortable with silence, took many deep breaths, and used the time to get grounded. It paid off; the deal went well."

—Barbara J. Krumsiek, president, CEO, and chair of Calvert Investments, Inc.

The second person should act as an observer and coach, stopping you at points to give you objective feedback and advice. For example, he or she might say, "You're talking too much and not letting your counterpart get a question in" or "The three reasons you just gave were compelling but you presented them in a shaky, unsure manner." This iterative process need not be done with subject matter experts on the topic of the negotiation. Having people poke holes in your argument and defending your stance will help you feel more confident and better equipped when it's actually time to sit down and bargain. Furthermore, the process of asking while getting instant feedback cuts through the fog and shows you exactly where you need to strengthen your argument.

GET IN THE MOOD

Could stubbing your toe getting out of bed and missing your train the same morning actually affect how you negotiate later that day? When it comes to our mood, research tells us that our mind-set going into a negotiation can in fact drive its outcomes. The Program on Negotiation, for example, a university consortium among Harvard University, Massachusetts Institute of Technology, and Tufts University, explains that one of the reasons negotiations are so difficult is that they "require us both to compete to *claim* value and to cooperate to *create* value."[7] On the one hand, it can feel like we're battling for a piece of the same pie; on the other hand, we're also looking to create new, unprecedented solutions that don't yet exist. The ability to swivel back and forth between these two goals, they explain, is an art, and a difficult one at that. Women in particular need to remember that rather than jumping right to value creation, we can and should linger on value claiming, even when it's uncomfortable.

Researchers Alice Isen and Peter Carnevale found that a positive mood actually leads to greater value creation in a negotiation. For example, an optimistic outlook can promote the idea that a conversation is low in risk. When we feel less defensive, and therefore safer in a tough conversation, we can bargain with more creativity, empathy, generosity, and resourcefulness.[8]

To help you build your sense of optimism, take the time to visualize the actual negotiation in your mind. I have used this strategy countless times for anxiety-producing events, and it has helped me in every instance. Instead of letting my mind go wherever it wants to before an important event like a negotiation, conference presentation, or sales pitch, I purposefully move myself to a quiet place where I can concentrate uninterrupted.

I slowly and purposefully picture myself presenting or negotiating with ease, speaking comfortably and confidently. I build on the image, picturing the person I am negotiating with seeing my point of view and respecting me for speaking up. I picture the outcome as I would like to see it, and I see myself after the negotiation feeling pride in myself for holding my ground. By taking the newness out of the situation through role-plays and visualization, you will clear your mind of fear and be better able to access your best ideas during the actual negotiation.

CHANNELING YOUR OWN EMOTIONS

As you identify where your emotions are when leading up to a negotiation, remember to use them to your advantage. You don't need to obliterate them; you just need to be aware of and identify them and see them as a form of energy. Fizzah Jafri, COO, Fixed Income Research and Economics at Morgan Stanley, suggests, "Women can be seen as not assertive enough. To guard against this, I write down exactly the way I plan to say something. I don't want to have a rambling, emotional response in a meeting where I lose my credibility and everyone in the room. I structure my thoughts and convey them so I keep everyone's attention. I try to be clear, drawing on the framework I've written out. Sometimes it's as simple as, 'Here's my request and here are ten reasons why I should get it.'"

Positive messages aside, even centering yourself and letting your mind go quiet can often be enough. "If I know I'm going into a tough conversation, I can get keyed up and feel emotional," offers DeeDee Wilson. "Then when I'm emotional, it tends to raise my counterpart's level of emotion, too, which in turn pushes my emotion up more. This is not good. To counteract it, I always try to get a good night's sleep before an important deal. I also meditate to get myself in a calm, introverted place."

What you discern, along with what you're willing to admit to or acknowledge, can position you favorably. See your emotional fortitude as being akin to the martial art of Aikido. Morihei Ueshiba, founder of Aikido, wanted to develop a martial art "that practitioners could use to defend themselves while also protecting their attacker from injury."[9] Aikido is performed by blending with the motion of the attacker and redirecting the force of the attack rather than opposing it head-on. This requires very little physical strength because the aikido practitioner "leads" the attacker's momentum using entering and turning movements. You, too, will grapple using yours and your opponent's potency. Remember then, your emotions and your opponents aren't a liability but necessary in your own self-defense.

LOOK FOR THE DUAL AGENDA

Outside of making certain that your emotions are in check and that your attitude is optimistic, I recommend that you approach negotiations with the mind-set that both parties can and will gain from the encounter. This dual agenda, in contrast to a singular win-lose style, reaches for mutually favorable outcomes that give as much of what both parties want as possible. In doing so, it often becomes clear that two counterparts' positions are not as diametrically opposed as they may have initially appeared.

DeeDee Wilson expands on this idea. "If the word *negotiation* invokes in you a 'me-versus-you' dynamic, I can guarantee you the conversation will be difficult. We women don't like conflict; negotiation smacks of two opposing sides. Look at it more as a conversation to come to a common decision. Frame it as 'I want to get to the best answer.' I personally like to assume a level of connection between my counterparts and me, trusting they also have the intent to come to a decision for the common good."

Negotiation Checklist: Psychological Preparation

Be certain to consider each of the factors and steps listed here as you ready yourself for your next negotiation:

- Acknowledge your negotiating roots, then focus on your new credo and approach.
- Select what the best negotiating style is for the situation at hand.
- Insist on balanced thinking, focusing on potentials costs and rewards.
- Regulate emotions by overpreparing your case.
- Key into your counterpart's goals, passions, and struggles.
- Engage mentors and note best practices.
- Identify what your leverage is in the negotiation.
- Role-play the negotiation at least once.
- Visualize successful outcomes.
- Dwell on past successes.
- Take a win-win approach: how can we both stand to gain?
- Don't underestimate or diminish your power.

Lucy S. Danziger, editor-in-chief of *SELF Magazine,* has a similar approach. "Look for common ground first, finding where you can both be happy. Uncover all the ways you can help each other, treating your counterpart as your partner, not your adversary. I will say, 'We're doing X together and it works. What if we did Y together?' . . . Everyone should hang up the phone or leave the meeting thinking, 'This is great, we're all going to do well in this deal.' Never leave people feeling like they've been taken."

Go For It!

Options will open up everywhere when we build a bridge from the everyday negotiations we already engage in to those in the workplace. The women I interviewed had over time developed a comfort and ease when it came to asking for what they want—necessarily, because being a leader often requires asking for tangible resources, more funds in the budget, another staff member, or advocating for an alternate direction for the organization. Even so, the women I met didn't become adept at negotiating by becoming hard or callous. Lucy S. Danziger shares, "I'm actually overly sensitive . . . . You don't have to be tough as nails to succeed at work. There will be times when you have to be willing to be unpopular. Everyone wants to be friends with colleagues and feel good, but allowing for disagreement can create much better outcomes in the end."

You do not need to love negotiating to do it, but understanding the psychological factors at play in any negotiation helps you do it more effectively. Expect emotions to be part of the negotiation dance and you won't be surprised when they accompany you into an important negotiation. If you feel the fear but negotiate anyway, you are far more likely to get what you want. If it feels uncomfortable, do it anyway. If you aren't totally prepared with every fact, do it anyway.

If it will call on interpersonal skills you don't have, do it anyway. If it goes badly, don't let that stop you. The success of each individual negotiation is less important than the overall goal: building a set of skills that will in time become second nature. Negotiation will almost never hurt you. Even when you don't win, you learn, and that's a process that should never end.

4

Do Your Homework

A funny thing happens when women arrive at the negotiating table having done their homework. They tend to come in to the room with a different confidence, sit with a little more authority, and argue their case unapologetically. When we take the time to gather key data before an important meeting, we supply ourselves with a well-equipped bench from which we can access tools as we need them, reacting with finesse and flexibility and pivoting as required. It's hard for that action not to have a positive, cascading effect on every aspect of our performance.

Consider what professional improvisers know. Whether comedians or musicians, these performers have to ad lib their way through a scene or song all the time. Although it may appear that they're merely channeling whatever's in their mind, in fact the process is much more structured than that. An improv comedian is extemporizing while operating within a set of rules and best practices. Guideposts such as, "Make your partner look good," "Tell a story," and "Don't refute another's idea" all help the comedian know how to react quickly and constructively. Similarly, many jazz musicians can free associate and improvise with an ensemble but those who are most successful are fluent in lots of musical styles and rules. Given their knowledge of many music idioms and theories, great jazz improvisers filter out what won't fit in a given song and can create within the rules of the style that does work. When you make a request of someone, it can be detrimental to let ideas flow haphazardly. Instead, I encourage you to think of your ideas as having a basic structure to them. The bones of your ask conversation can be replicated with different counterparts and imply that you will have some control over the pace and direction of the conversation. By framing the conversation with an overarching, cooperation-inducing statement, followed by thoughtfully making the ask, we set ourselves up well to then substantiate the key points of our argument with evidence. Following these steps, it's critical to follow up and thank our counterpart.

Although we'll look at the phases of maneuvering through a negotiation on game day more closely in Chapter Five, I want to be sure you have the necessary preparation done so that the substantiating phase is pain free and seamless.

Similarly, you will do your best pushback work if you have data points and a clear argument, which can be used much like guideposts within your reach. Yes, you'll need quick reflexes, too, but you don't need to be a magician if you take the time in advance to create a framework for spontaneity. "When you see really impressive people in a business discussion, it's not necessarily that they're the best egg in the basket. It's more likely that they're the most prepared. That concept is a very simple—yet very underestimated—one," advises Rosemary Turner, president of Chesapeake UPS.

So that's your ultimate goal: the ability to create a framework for improvisation in a negotiation. When you can do this, you're like a musician or athlete performing at a high level. Your skills flower and you do your very best work. In Chapter Five, we'll talk about tactics and strategies for game day—the conversation itself. Here we're going to talk about how you build the structure beforehand.

A TIERED APPROACH TO PREPARATION

Your best approach to preparing for an important ask or difficult conversation is a tiered one. This means you're not going into the room without considering the short-term *and* long-term implications of your ask, the one-on-one relationship with your counterpart *and* various other dynamics in the organization. The good news is that there is a method to this approach, with five replicable tiers or steps:

- *Step One:* Gather the tangibles.
- *Step Two:* Get in their heads.
- *Step Three:* Enlist your network.
- *Step Four:* Choose strategies and a style.
- *Step Five:* Prepare to tell the story.
- *Step Six:* Nail down the logistics.

All the tiers of preparation matter; on their own, the parts are not nearly as powerful as they are together. Before you know it, you'll be moving through the phases in an intuitive way that you can repeat all the time in all kinds of negotiation situations.

Step One: Gather the Tangibles

Although you shouldn't disregard a gut feeling before making an ask, don't rely on instinct to provide you with enough information to make a case. In the business world, the more you can ground your argument in information that's hard to refute, the more airtight your case. The hardest information to poke holes in is usually factual, quantifiable, or historical in nature. Future-looking information, such as projections, can also be persuasive, depending on who has done the analysis and their level of credibility.

In business school, my professors corrected us every time we made a case or point starting with "I think," "I feel," or "I believe." "Stick with verifiable information," they urged us, "and you'll find that people can criticize your argument much less." Fizzah Jafri, COO, Fixed Income Research and Economics at Morgan Stanley, built on this idea, noting, "I start [making a case] by getting a lot of data: costs, numbers, turnover; anything impacting the end decision. This tangible information makes you sound smart. If you think about it, it's just like writing a paper in school. Your opinion matters, but only in the context of the research you've done."

So just what types of data are helpful? Anything numeric, research-based, or showing a precedent can help to meaningfully bolster your case. If none of these exist, then the onus on you is greater to demonstrate the potential of your idea. The following summarizes some of the most commonly used items you can draw on in a pushback conversation:

- *Analytical data:* Profit-and-loss statements, future projections, costs, revenues, repeat business, cost of inaction, industry benchmarks, SWOT (strengths, weakness, opportunities, and threats) analysis, cost-benefit analysis, sales potential, return on investment, research studies, and surveys
- *People data:* Performance levels, departmental or other turnover, promotion rates, employee engagement scores, workload data, comparative data across departments, tenure, employee utilization rates, pay scales, praise, or accolades
- *Contextual data and benchmarks:* Information about successful past initiatives at the company or successful initiatives at competitor companies, cautionary tales from competitor

companies, unsuccessful past initiatives at the company, larger trends, and changes in the industry

As you go about the process of collecting data, I urge you to be creative. The more data you have from persuasive sources, the better. While getting my MBA from Johns Hopkins University, for example, I was readying to ask my boss for a sizeable raise. I had collected information on my performance, along with data from Salary.com, an industry association compensation report, and internal pay scales.

Around the same time, the director of my MBA program did a survey gauging the salaries of the students. The answers were to be anonymous and would be averaged into an aggregate for the school's admissions data. When I asked the MBA director for the overall results, he was happy to share them with me even if I wasn't happy with what I read; I found that I was paid less than other members of my MBA class by a substantial margin.

Frustrated—but motivated—I decided I'd include this figure in my case because it supported my point, even if I didn't lead with it. While pushing back on the status quo and presenting every data point I had, my boss listened quietly. She finally said, "I'll give you the 20 percent raise you're asking for now and I'll give you 5 percent more six months from now. I want you to stick around." I was overjoyed! I finally understood the principle that people had been telling me for years: "You don't get what you don't ask for." Is there an unturned rock you can look for, a place where no one's yet sought information? Be a detective and look in even untraditional areas for useful information. The following list offers some common examples of metrics and their applications to everyday asking conversations.

Common Data Points	
Requesting a flexible work arrangement: • Performance metrics • Percent of other employees with current flexible arrangements • Data on increased productivity resulting from flexible arrangements • Competitor data regarding flexible arrangements	Negotiating for a phase-back maternity leave (returning to work on an adjusted, graduated schedule): • Current policy including strengths and limitations • Added costs, if any, of phase-back leave • Current employer-of-choice status versus potential improved status • Competitor data regarding maternity leaves • Analysis of workload and employee utilization for new arrangement
Negotiating for a not-yet-existent job at your company: • Performance metrics • Proof of your candidacy to perform tasks • Level of reliance on and need for the tasks you plan to perform • Increased demand of your skills within the company • Other positive precedents set with people getting newly developed roles	Asking for a raise: • Performance metrics • Praise and accolades • Level of reliance on the tasks you perform • Salary benchmarks • Industry or association salary data • Competitor data on compensation • Current and potential needs within the company
Requesting a larger professional development budget: • Performance metrics • Return on investment of training • Demonstration of how new skills will benefit company, department, and your boss • How you plan to share the learning you gain with others	Asking for an assistant or increased headcount: • Departmental performance metrics • Current and potential needs within the department • Typical assistant arrangements within the company (level of seniority, revenue generated, etc.) • Benchmarking: how competitors configure their work units and the employment of assistants

Creating a Baseline

One of the most simple yet most effective ways to leverage data is by creating a baseline. A baseline is more than just a hunch on how things are in a given department or on a project; a baseline illustrates accurately *how things actually look now.* If the saying is true that you can't change what you don't measure, baseline data can give you a starting place to establish credibility and then build an argument for change.

By baselining your team's productivity, for example, you will often demonstrate deeper knowledge of the subject matter than your counterpart. Let's say you are asking for a temporary worker to be brought in during your department's approaching busy season. Be prepared by coming in with a current snapshot of what you're facing. "As you know, we're currently servicing 350 customers a week and we're able to manage that volume comfortably. Judging by last year's figures, though, that number should double starting in March. Given that trend, I'm asking for a temporary worker to come in before our busiest point, in late February."

Data is a hard-to-match weapon. By weaving it into your dialogue, you can lessen your counterpart's defenses and neutralize the conversation. Don't leverage only your knowledge of and intimacy with the facts and numbers in a pushback situation, go out and get new data yourself. Often the data point we need to seal our case is something out of reach or that doesn't exist. If you're pressing for changes to the maternity leave plan, for example, then why not offer to colead a focus group asking women what they want most in a parental leave plan? By doing so you'll have control over the data collection process and, as in the next example, you'll be able to convince others.

On Creating Your Own Evidence

"I'm in charge of the creative look and feel of our sports networks. Years ago before digital media, we didn't put a ticker at the bottom of the television screen during sports matches showing the score. The thinking was that people wouldn't stay tuned during the whole game if we always showed the score.

I argued unsuccessfully for including a more dynamic ticker. One year, when we were doing our annual survey of viewers, I added questions about the ticker. It emerged as one of the four most important things to viewers during our programming. I needed irrefutable research and when it wasn't available, I found a way to collect the data. These data provided the proof of value needed, and the more dynamic ticker was added to our networks."

— April Carty-Sipp, SVP of Creative Services, Comcast Sports Group

Take a moment to consider a negotiation you'd like to initiate and how you could support that request. On a piece of a paper write, "What I'm negotiating for...." List exactly what it is you'd like to get from a negotiation; for example, *I want to work one day a week from home* or *I want a $5,000 raise.* Now write on the paper, "Sources of supporting evidence I'll seek out ... " List the research you'll need to do to support your request—for example, relevant human resources policy, precedents elsewhere in the company, salary surveys of your industry, and so on.

Think Strategically

You'll give yourself an advantage on game day if you have taken the time to see the problem with some long-term insight. Why? People tend to acquiesce and be persuaded by official or unofficial leaders, those individuals who have, among other traits, visionary and strategic thinking rather than just tactical thinking. Tactical workers, by contrast, are focused on right now. The tactical worker sees disparate parts, the strategic leader projects into the future, trying to get a wider perspective on a matter. Resist the urge to just fix something affecting today; instead, look at what practices are spoken and unspoken and take a minute to step back from the close-up view. Here are some examples of tactical versus strategic approaches to the same issue:

Tactical Perspective	Strategic Perspective
Sandy gave her resignation. I'd like to start a search to replace her role immediately.	With Sandy leaving, I'd like to reassess the needs of our department and possibly rewrite her job description. I'm not convinced that the structure of Sandy's role best met our needs in the first place.
There's a bottleneck in our proposal-writing system. Let's fix that blockage so proposals can be sent out more quickly.	Given the proposal demands we have today, plus those we're expecting in the near future, I'd like to look at our entire proposal writing process and see how it can be made more agile and efficient.
The new diversity taskforce has attracted low numbers of members. There must not be enough interest in the group.	The diversity taskforce isn't as large as we'd hoped, but by looking outside of the firm, I'm sure we can find some helpful best practices to increase our membership numbers.
I understand that I didn't place my order in time for us to get our graphics next week. Is there any way you can make an exception just this once?	I keep finding myself on a short deadline to get graphics. Can you and I get creative and think about how we can work in a different way, one that's quick and efficient for both of us?

In short, if you want to transcend surface discussion—and make a far more convincing, thoughtful case—you'll connect how your ask interrelates with other parts of the business. By actively looking for ripple or domino effects and using them as part of your forecasts, you show that you've considered the larger system, and you'll preempt criticism or pushback.

Step Two: Get in Their Heads

Why does the psychology of the other person matter in a negotiation? Because the way your counterparts relate to the world can and will affect their reaction to whatever you're asking for. No, you can't understand all of the forces that affect how someone operates in the world, but there's considerable information right in front of us that can be used as conversation "gold" in a negotiation.

Taking the time to think about where your counterparts are mentally and emotionally, along with contextual factors such as workload or current demands, will give you more of the crucial data you need to be successful pushing back. "I encourage young women never to take negotiations personally and to always conduct themselves in a professional manner. Listen carefully, respond to what is actually being said, and always try to look through the other person's eyes before responding. If you do that well, you'll significantly improve the chances of a very successful outcome," offers Cindi Bigelow, president of Bigelow Tea. Sometimes the last thing we want to do is empathize with the other side and yet that's exactly what gives us more power to get what we want.

Sheila Murphy, associate general counsel at MetLife, recalls a specific strategy she uses to get in her counterpart's head. "When I don't know the individual I'll be negotiating with, I reach out to people in my network to see how my counterpart operates. Sometimes it's even appropriate to bring your mutual connection into the negotiation." Learning about your counterpart through others is a low-risk, yet high-yield activity. Don't make the mistake of involving only one person. Instead, get broad, well-rounded knowledge from different people.

Carol Ann Petren, executive vice president and general counsel, MacAndrews & Forbes Holdings Inc., suggests, "It's important that you know the person across the table, and more particularly, that person's perspective and pressure points. Spending time to understand what makes that person tick will position you well in getting to a resolution more quickly." Carol's astute point about forces can be broken down even further. Relationship specialist Ed Wallace, author of *Business Relationships That Last*, urges those trying to persuade others to think beyond their counterpart's pains or problems. Ed says that every one of our counterpart's needs will fall under one of these three categories:

- *Goals:* Personal short- and long-term business objectives
- *Passions:* Business and personal causes people care deeply about
- *Struggles:* Obstacles or commitments that are holding them back[1]

Every time you get prepared for a pushback situation, consider your counterpart's goals, passions, and struggles. Let's say you're about to ask if your tuition can be covered by the firm for "green" or environmental training. Knowing that your boss is responsible within his goals for making the company more efficient, could you offer to do an internal assessment of energy efficiency following the training? Perhaps your writing a CliffsNotes version of the class will help your boss and become part of the terms of your request. If your counterpart is passionate about sustainability, can you somehow make your request include or touch on that issue? Could you offer to advance that initiative within the company?

It shouldn't be hard to put your finger on one of your counterpart's struggles. Let's say, for example, that you want more responsibility. You've noticed that your boss, who is responsible for circulating projections every month, circulates minimal information in his report. You might offer to do further data analysis on the figures each month, better equipping everyone who receives the report. If such an activity is your specialty or is otherwise easy for you to do, how could offering your own services to alleviate a struggle *not* add a new dimension to the conversation? To be sure, not every goal, passion, or struggle will be furthered or fixed by your ask. But if you can key into these three sets of issues, you will more often bolster and advance your cause than not.

On Learning That Language Matters

"Knowing your business builds credibility, as does knowing the facts of the issue. Speak your counterpart's language! Early in my career, I took a hit because I spoke to a specialty business unit referencing old vocabulary and terms that they no longer used. That really eroded my credibility in their eyes. I took that experience as a prompt to partner with someone who knew the business better than I did."

—Sheila Murphy, associate general counsel at MetLife

More personal, stylistic information about your counterpart is also very valuable. Try to find out information by answering the following questions:

- How does my counterpart like to be communicated with?
- Who or what does my counterpart tend to endorse?
- Who or what does my counterpart tend to object to?
- Why has my counterpart not taken the action I'm about to request? What's contributing to that inaction?
- What is my counterpart's dominant communication style? Does he or she favor a quantitative, feeling-centric, anecdotal, or analytical approach?
- What do I know about how my counterpart processes information? What is his or her process for arriving at decisions?
- What action can I take to make saying yes easier for my counterpart?

You should be able to collect most of this data by simply observing those you work with in meetings, e-mails, and even hallway conversation. Is your counterpart curt and to the point when speaking? Then you may want to take a similar approach. Is your counterpart a stickler for evidence and needs proof to accept new ideas? Then prepare accordingly.

We know from social psychology that similarity is one of the strongest indicators of likeability. When people display similar behaviors to our own, we may be more likely to agree with them because their behavior is validating our own modus operandi (MO). Successful salespeople have known this for years, often parroting the person they are selling to in body language, tone, even in conversation style. When we take this approach, we're communicating, "I'm not that dissimilar to you. You can trust my judgment."

Finally, you should prepare for a tough conversation by confirming that the person you're negotiating with is in fact in a position to act as a decision maker. Learning about your counterparts and getting in their heads means understanding what scope their authority includes. If your counterparts aren't empowered to make a decision, be certain they have enough influence to at least be your advocate.

Step Three: Enlist Your Network

What do you suppose is the most underused tool in a negotiation? If you answered "my network," you're right. Your network can offer you many kinds of help, from giving insight into your counterpart's motivations and style to acting as sounding boards, test markets, or even sponsors of your initiative. Do not neglect this rich source of perspective and support.

The people you consult in connection with a situation should think differently than you and have a different perspective of the situation. As Karen Ganzlin, chief human resources officer at TD

Ameritrade, astutely notes, "If two people always agree, then one isn't needed." A smart peer or mentor can do more than boost your confidence; he or she can see a dynamic you don't or glean a conclusion before you do.

The Main Ask and the Backdoor Ask

"Recently we were looking at what functions we prioritize as a company. I felt uncomfortable with where my team, accounting, was positioned. We were effectively stuck in the middle of other functions, working as traffic cops. I stepped back and asked, 'Who—if I got their support—would bring along others? Who could help us be seen differently?' I went to others, asking for their best ideas. The main 'ask' is for ideas, but the backdoor 'ask' is for their support. You can tell by how people engage with you in the 'ideas' conversation how much they support you."

—Susan McFarland, executive vice president and principal accounting officer
at Capital One

Linda Descano, president and CEO of Women & Co., a program of Citibank, also credits consultations as having helped her. "I ask other people for pushback on my presentation and think from a cynical standpoint, 'How will my pitch or idea be received?' I leverage my network and ask people I trust what, in particular, I should pay attention to.... Once, when I reached out to a colleague for advice on a negotiation with a man, she advised, 'The best thing you can do is interrupt him within the first five minutes. He'll see it as a sign of strength.' I did what she recommended and it worked. Your network can help you uncover small but important nuances like that."

Asking a selection of your colleagues and peers about a negotiation is smart practice. You will inevitably get more information than you started with, you'll benefit from diversity of thought, and you'll be strengthening your own network relationships along the way. Don't forget that people are often flattered when you seek out their counsel. By asking, "Who here has successfully negotiated something? How did you position your ask?" you may just end up discovering an existing viable template. Working your relationships before an important ask can also be politically astute. "I work in a role where it's important to spend a lot of time influencing," notes Deborah Simpson, chief financial officer of The Boston Consulting Group. "At my firm, there's a high bar on being able to debate effectively and convey the benefits of your idea. You need to ask, 'Who can I get on board in advance?' It's not just about saying the right thing at the meeting."

To avoid triangulating or coming across in a gossipy way, keep your consultations constructive. The last thing you want when you enlist your network is to convey that you attack people behind their backs or complain. Keep your language positive—for example, "I know you've worked with Jack in operations before. I really want to find a win-win solution when he and I negotiate about where the compliance group will move. What have you found works well in dealing with him?"

Nuances abound in negotiations. By arming yourself with information about your counterpart, you give yourself the tools to be agile and to find an approach that will work in each situation. "With some people you can make your case directly while with others it may be better to position it as their idea," notes Carol Ann Petren. "In other cases, I find it serves me to be quite direct." These are the kind of small but powerful insights that separate a successful from an unsuccessful negotiation; gathering such insights before you sit down at the table is part of savvy preparation.

Your Sounding Board

Be strategic about approaching people to gather data. Although there might be some individuals you can share all of your hopes and fears with, others should be engaged in a more contained way. Such people can serve as a sounding board for you—one or more people external to your cause who can share critical feedback. "I'll float the idea to gauge initial reactions with individuals who won't be involved in the final outcome," shares Lori A. Greenawalt, partner at KPMG LLP. "I do this to make sure I'm seeing both the pros and cons; after all, I might not know the whole political infrastructure at play. If I get some pushback, I'll say, 'Let me look into it more.'"

Your sounding board can be especially effective at seeing things you can't. They can often easily slide empathically from your position to your counterpart's, seeing both sides of the issue. These consultations can also yield important information such as obvious counterarguments or the larger context or picture.

Socialize Your Ideas

Another way you might like to engage your network is by testing your ideas out on them. Planting seeds with your counterparts may help to make the real conversation or meeting go more smoothly. Look at what it will take for the person to be receptive to hearing your request; it is often not good strategy to take your counterpart by surprise. Rebecca Baker, chief marketing officer and global partner, Alvarez & Marsal, notes, "When you spring a request on someone, you put them at a disadvantage. . . . Learn the MO of the person you're meeting with. Sometimes I'll even say outright, 'I need to talk to you about X topic and I have an ask I need to make. How would you like to proceed?' They'll often tell me they want something to read to get familiar with the topic first. Other times they'll ask me on the spot to spit it out. Set yourself up to win at making your request and set them up to win at saying 'yes' to your request." Peers and former coworkers can greatly help in advancing your cause but nothing can match the power of sponsors.

> ### The Sponsor Effect
>
> Much ado has been made about the importance of sponsors (as contrasted with mentors) in the career advancement of women. Although mentors are seen as the friendly guides who dispense helpful information, sponsors are generally more powerful. Sponsors have the willingness and ability to open doors. They will personally advocate for a cause on your behalf. I'd argue that we need the learning from mentors to survive and the advocacy of sponsors to get what we need.
>
> Economist Sylvia Ann Hewlett, in her report "The Sponsor Effect," notes that "women underestimate the power of the sponsor effect. Sponsorship confers a statistical benefit of up to 30 percent in terms of more stretch assignments, promotions, and pay raises." Hewlett goes on to cite key examples of the sponsor effect, including President Obama's advocacy of Elena Kagan or John McCain's sponsorship of Sarah Palin.[2]

Test-marketing your idea with the group or a subset of the group can also help you perform better on game day. "Once I have data, I send an e-mail to my counterparts with the numbers, showing my rationale before we meet. If something doesn't look right, I invite them to comment. This saves me embarrassment in a meeting if my information is incorrect or incomplete," says Fizzah Jafri, from direct experience.

Karen Ganzlin continues this concept: " ... I spend a lot of time socializing ideas. What I've learned over the years is that no one likes to be surprised.... I'll explain my approach and ask, 'Have you got a different read? Is there something I haven't considered?'

I work on a no-surprise type of basis." You can include people incrementally in your plan, via e-mail and in-person meetings, or through many other combinations and formats. In doing so, you'll need to gauge your environment, workplace culture, and most of all, your counterpart if you want to move others to do it your way.

A sponsor, if you have one in a position to do so, can grease the wheels, giving your cause added momentum. In calling on sponsors, though, you'll want to operate with proper etiquette in mind to keep the relationship intact. Lori A. Greenawalt notes, "When I approach sponsors—which is essentially calling on the clout of others—I'll spread the credit for the project to them as well. Even if they made an intangible contribution, I give them recognition. This really helps the next time you have a request." In the best scenarios, sponsors are people you can regularly approach for counsel and support. See the relationship in a long-term way and you'll tend to take care of it with an eye toward longevity and sustainability.

Step Four: Choose Strategies and a Style

The negotiation strategies and style that we choose have a bearing on the relationship we have or hope to develop with the other party. This means that the tactics and methods we employ—as well as the tone and manner we communicate with—will affect our counterparts and their willingness to see it our way. Too many inexperienced negotiators put all of their effort into attempts to repeatedly convince the other side of their argument. You've probably been in a similar fight—a contentious discussion where you and your counterpart disagree and your counterpart continues to restate the main message over and again. This one-dimensional style of negotiating is seldom the best choice; it alienates others, hammering home "I want to be right," rather than "I want to find a mutually beneficial agreement."

As you think about which tactics to employ, it can help to know the extremes that exist and certainly the middle ground in between. Which approach will you use when you're preparing for your next ask or tough conversation?

Pushback Approaches on a Continuum			
Evidence	**Data**	**Resoluteness**	**Demeanor**
• Hypothesis driven • Observation or perception based • Anecdotal	• Qualitative • Deals with descriptions and observations but not measurement	• Open • Flexible • Several right outcomes	• Emotion, feeling, or sentiment based • Humanizes the situation
Versus			
• Fact based • Proven • Documented	• Quantitative • Deals with that which can be measured	• Unyielding • Firm • One right outcome	• Logical • Emphasizes analytical lens

As you create a tailored approach to work with your counterpart, you'll find that you can potentially call on all kinds of styles. In some cases, when you know you might be steamrolled by a person, you'll want to purposely take a firmer, more unyielding stance. At times you'll want to fortify your case with numbers. At other times you'll need to humanize what you're asking for; for example, imagine there's backlash to a new time-reporting system that's been put into place at your company. As you push back, you might vary your argument. Starting with what *is* working or positive, you might say, "All fifty of my direct reports are now using the new reporting system. They are clocking in and out at every break from work.

The issue though, Tom, is that people are feeling like they're being watched—like they're not trustworthy. We're happy to help get you workload data but I have concerns about the message that the current approach is sending."

Thinking through your approach means asking, "What will make this argument the most persuasive to my counterpart?" Each approach has merit on its own and can be employed situationally or as an ensemble. Through experience, you'll be able to see when you've effectively prepared and embodied a style or when you would have been better served to tailor your style further to your counterpart. You'll also invent additional categories (not listed here) that allow you to convey your points, be heard, and get what you need.

Lucy S. Danziger, editor-in-chief of *SELF Magazine,* takes selecting a style one step further: " . . . If I anticipate pushback, I'll first have an offline conversation with that person. It doesn't behoove you to go toe-to-toe in a group meeting. If you do, someone's going to look bad, either you as a bully or them, appearing as though they lack authority or have been slapped down. If you want someone's opinion, offer to take them to breakfast or bring them to your office and ask what they're thinking. Nail down where the resistance is coming from by simply asking, 'What's making you not want to move forward?' If I see a viable path forward, part of my job is to help others get there." Indeed in preparing for a negotiation and choosing a style and a strategy, you will train yourself not to go into these conversations using the same tactics with everyone but to mold your content to the person at hand.

Prework: Take the World on Your Shoulders

An important part of many asks becomes, "Who's going to do the work needed to make this happen?" If you're proposing a new product be designed and introduced to the market, who will staff the project and how much will it cost? The answers to these questions represent the bare minimum of what we must know before asking. Lori A. Greenawalt cites, "When making a case for something, it's key to be prepared to do the majority of the work involved."

The Harvard Negotiation Project has studied how negotiators can gain an edge when they're in the seemingly weak position of negotiating with a busy group or a powerful bureaucracy. The research group recommends that you present the other side with a draft agreement that authorizes or approves your request. By doing so, busy decision makers who lack details of your plan instantly have them at hand. What's more, your counterpart is likely to see your prework as a time-saver. The Harvard Negotiation Project explains that this savvy approach is called on by Washington lobbyists, who often draft the laws they want to see enacted when proposing ideas to congressional staff.[3]

Although we can't always draft a document with a signature line, we can take on the prework of drafting plans. The following asking scenarios show how offering up a persuasive tangible document right from the outset of the conversation can be used.

Request	Prework
I want to work a reduced, thirty-hour-a-week schedule.	A work plan that shows how your work will be managed and accomplished and who will provide coverage when you're not in the office
I'm proposing a new job at my firm that doesn't yet exist.	A draft job description that lays out the needed competencies, responsibilities, contributions, and authority of the role
I'm asking the firm to cover my tuition for graduate school.	A sample agreement laying out the exact terms of the tuition reimbursement deal and its effect on subsequent employment
I'd like the office to provide lactation rooms for working mothers.	A work plan that recommends the number of rooms needed along with proposed spaces

When you're asking for something unprecedented, pushing for a controversial initiative, or going against the culture of your workplace, the quality of your prework becomes even more important. In these situations, you're asking people to use their imaginations to envision what only you can see. For example, if you want to create a job-sharing program at your office that has not been attempted, your counterpart will be thinking, "Why do this now? Where do our competitors sit on this issue? What are the potential downsides?" Squarely responding to such questions before they arise will show that you recognize the newness of what you're proposing. This is an instance when it's clearly important to anticipate your counterpart's concerns and motivations.

Arming Yourself with Data

You also need to be equipped with data about your record of performance and be prepared to take on a lot of the legwork to implement your vision once you've got the green light. Lori A. Greenawalt notes, "If you want to ask for something unprecedented, you must be a consistent and exceptional performer. You'll need to articulate the value of the change you're proposing. It helps to be willing to create rules and structures and to be realistic about success or failure. If the company is going to make an accommodation for you—going out on a limb to do it your way—then they must have faith in your abilities and know you have a commitment to make it work."

Creating a work plan or sample agreement can be one way to show your commitment to making a new arrangement work. Don't be afraid to create a scaffolding for an initiative, especially if it's a new one. "Shift your request from 'I want' to 'This is what I'm proposing and these are the benefits it could bring,'" suggests Irene Chang Britt, chief strategy officer at Campbell Soup Company. "Paint a vivid picture of how your idea or change will look once implemented. Begin by framing how it will help the company first, how it will help the business or functional group second, how it will help the person you're asking next, and finally, how it will help you. Always make things easy for people and be willing to do the bulk of the work."

Step Five: Prepare to Tell the Story

Your final preparation step is to take all that you've amassed and turn it into a compelling story. How will the case you're making actually spur action—how will it move the people you are engaging?

Business leaders agree: story really matters when you are trying to persuade. Peter Guber's best-selling book, *Tell to Win*, describes how telling compelling stories has the power to move partners, shareholders, customers, and employees to action. Gruber believes that if you move your listeners' hearts, their feet and wallets will follow. Gruber's most astute pointer states, "Story isn't the icing on the cake, it is the cake."[4]

Linda Descano endorses storytelling also. "I'm all about preparation. I put together a story that has a beginning, middle, and end. I really try to understand the audience or individuals and then deliver my story to fit their needs." In thinking through your performance prior to game day, think of ways you can connect with your counterpart rather than just inundating him or her with information. Similarly, avoid expecting perfection of yourself and instead focus on making a connection and finding mutually beneficial overlap. The best storytellers tend to be highly empathetic: showing that they know what their audience cares about makes their stories feel much more relevant.

Storytelling: Structure and Tactics

Fortunately you do not have to invent the wheel each time you craft a story—there are tried-and-true formulas you can use and tactics that can help you stay on message.

Journalists—who are in the story-writing business—use a formula like this to craft a convincing article:

Lead (Hook) → Thesis → Evidence → Preempt Objections → Conclusion[5]

This formula wasn't created at random; it tends to work because it pulls us in, provokes our interest, makes a case, establishes credibility, and anticipates criticism. You can use this structure for your story. How can you hook your audience, getting them engaged from the start? Similarly, how can you word your argument so that your key argument is made clearly and then is buttressed by evidence? A truly great storyteller takes the time to respond to obvious counterarguments or naysayers, then wraps everything up in a well-wrought, inevitable-seeming conclusion.

There is another useful model for structuring your story. Research shows that the order of what you say in a negotiation has a bearing on the outcome, showing that it matters *when* you make your important points. According to the serial position effect, we register and recall items differently, depending on their order. If people are offered a list of words, for example, they are most likely to remember the last words best (the recency effect), followed by the first few words (the primacy effect). Those words positioned in the middle of the list are hardest to recall.[6]

What can we learn from this? For one, we want to be sure that our most vital messages are delivered in introducing and even more so in concluding our meeting. Knowing that people tend to ascribe greater importance or significance to an opening or conclusion, we can leverage those facts, using them to our best advantage. This is not to say that our middle messages should be fluff, but you can propose items in the middle that a person can easily go back and reference later in a document. The following example depicts a typical negotiation flow:

Beginning	"I'd like to talk about my future here at the company. I've learned so much over the last three years and enjoy my work. I want to discuss how I can assume more responsibility."
Middle	"By managing the Miller, Syeed, and Benson accounts, I've gotten firsthand experience with clients—I've summarized them for you in this table that you can reference later. I'm asking to build on those experiences by taking a more senior role on the team, with more time interfacing with clients. I've drafted what a position like this could entail, in case you'd like to review it."
End	"Again, I want to be sure you know how appreciative I am of the learning opportunities I've gotten here. I'm committed to the firm and hope that you and I can find a way to broaden my responsibilities."

Use the primacy and recency effects to your advantage. Prepackage your messages so that they draw on what's really important and boost those points strategically in the beginning and end. Don't be afraid to reference materials or pieces that can be looked at or reviewed outside of the negotiation. Once you adopt this style and prepare your points in this way, you'll find it works well outside of negotiations—in sales pitches, presentations, or meetings, for example.

Lead the Witness

In law, a "leading question" is one in which the query itself suggests the answer. Although this is frowned on in many courtrooms, it remains a critical influencing tactic in other domains such as negotiation. "I make sure I know my audience," says April Carty-Sipp. "I get them behind my idea by carefully packaging it and selling it specifically to them. I tend to 'lead the witness,' meaning that if there are four or five choices and I like one the best, I make my choice really shine." Putting forth other viable options—different from your preferred one—shows that you've really thought through your matter. You are not looking at it in a narrow, one-sided way. On the contrary, you're aware of different viewpoints and have information on each, showing why they're less effective than your proposal.

Use Headlines

To keep yourself on point in a negotiation, consider drafting up headlines rather than detailed notes or a full-on script. These headlines should summarize your key points and prompt you to elaborate further verbally. If negotiating with a prospective employer on the benefits package in your offer, you might have the following headlines:

- I'm Thrilled You Made an Offer
- The Job Is Ideally Suited to Me
- I Still Have Some Concerns
- I'd Like Four Weeks of Vacation Time
- Research from A, B, and C Substantiates My Request

Headlines have a way of clearing away what's not important and helping you zero in on your key messages. As you craft your story, create headlines to keep your notes and reference materials clean and clear—and to keep you on point when you are at the negotiating table.

Step Six: Nail Down the Logistics

Rarely do we learn in school a critical element of influencing others and negotiating successfully: logistics! These little details such as how we present ourselves physically and the venue or what time of day we choose for a negotiation can still make a difference.

Preparing for the Little Things

A small but still important aspect of a negotiation is how you look and carry yourself on the day. Dressing in a way that helps you feel strong, credible, and powerful can telegraph those feelings into the actual negotiation. Ask yourself, "When have I felt my best in terms of presentation? What was I doing, wearing, or conveying when that happened?"

"I wear what I call 'warrior suits' on days when I know I'll have tough conversations," recalls Linda Descano. "I also wear lower heels than usual because I feel steadier on my feet and have a longer stride when I swagger into the room. These small things can give me more confidence. I also sit forward, more than I usually would, leaning in toward my counterpart."

Catherine Ann Mohan, partner and treasurer at McCarter & English, talks about women and appearance, including the expectations put on females versus males. "As someone who does lots of negotiating, I've found that people generally want professional women to look the part. I always dress professionally. A guy can walk in and be taken seriously with food on his tie, but if a woman's jacket doesn't go perfectly with her skirt, she'll be penalized. I once won a case in Maryland and my codefendant got hit for $15 million. I was the only woman in the courtroom. Afterwards, the jurors said to me, 'Every morning we chatted and wondered, what is Ms. Mohan going to wear today? We really liked how you accessorized.' I was baffled—that after winning a verdict like I did—they were talking about my appearance." Knowing that your physical presentation speaks before you do, plan your attire and remember what your audience is accustomed to.

An overlooked consideration in preparing for a negotiation is to know in advance certain nuts and bolts: attendance, venue, format, schedule, and agenda. Sometimes you'll be in control of these factors, sometimes you may be able to influence them, and sometimes they will be out of your hands. In any event, always be aware of them. For example, will your meeting be held with a group or one-on-one? Will attendees be physically present or remote? Could you have a mix of both? Is this a multipart conversation or is the hope that a resolution will be found today?

If you're presented with a choice of an in-person versus phone or e-mail exchange, always choose the in-person version. Body language is a major giveaway in negotiations and one that you want to use to your advantage when it comes to reading your counterpart. In a face-to-face meeting you also have more of a chance of coming across as a real person, with real needs, rather than just a counterpart.

If you must negotiate virtually, telephone is preferable to e-mail. You can ask your counterpart to use Skype or another video conferencing vehicle to bring the conversation to life and retain a face-to-face element.

The downside of resorting to e-mail is that everything said is in writing, up for interpretation, and at times can lack context. That leaves lots of opening for misunderstandings. E-mail communications can also remain relatively surface, making it hard to access true interests rather than superficial positions. *Scientific American* published a study that shows people are more likely to lie over e-mail than when writing things down with pencil and paper. The authors suggest that "e-mail is a young phenomenon and its social rules are looser and still evolving, whereas when you put something in writing, psychologically there is a stronger hold—it's really there, in writing."[7]

Still, plenty of deals have been worked out using an online format. You can guard against gross misunderstandings by keeping your language neutral, clear, and to the point. Also avoid e-mailing about highly sensitive or confidential matters, realizing that others can easily be copied, forwarded, or shown your e-mail correspondence.

Professor Markus Baer at Washington University in St. Louis conducted a study entitled, "Location in Negotiation: Is There a Home Field Advantage?" In it, he found that "parties who negotiate on their home field can be expected to claim between 60 percent and 160 percent more value than the visiting party."[8] If you are negotiating with a vendor, a client, even a boss, try if you can to hold the meeting at your own business or in your own office.

Timing

The timing of a meeting can influence its shape and outcome in a number of ways. Is there an important town hall assembly that you want your meeting to dovetail? Is there a certain time when you're more likely to have your counterpart's attention? Is your counterpart perpetually late, shortening meetings? "If I have one hour on someone's calendar, I might actually only get thirty minutes with that person. That's important to know," advises Linda Descano.

Lots of research suggests the optimal timing for making a request so that you have the best chance of having it accepted. The bottom line from this data? You want your counterparts to feel their best physically and their most optimistic and open mentally. So, don't ask when people are most groggy. Don't schedule a negotiation right before lunch (rumbling stomachs) or at the end of the day when your counterparts are distracted or may be tempted to hurry through the conversation.

When you finish an important project, you are often well positioned to ask for something. The same thing goes for repeat business you brought back or saving the company money. When is your boss generally experiencing the least stress? Use this insight to determine the best time of day to ask.

Timing factors

- Recent accomplishments or mistakes
- Your counterpart's mood
- Time of day realities (hunger, grogginess, etc.)
- The company's financial health or stability
- Relevant industry news

ASKING IS ALSO ABOUT CONCEDING ... OR IS IT?

You've prepared a justification for what you deserve and you're clear on how you'll ask for it. But have you considered what you might need to give up? Many of us need to be ready to give up something in order to get ahead in a negotiation.

You can prepare for the possibility of conceding by creating a list of options.

Sample List of Options		
• *Option A (most preferred)* • 10 percent raise		
	• *Option B* • 8 percent raise • Tuition reimbursement for a $1,000 course	
		• *Option C (least preferred)* • 6 percent raise • Four extra days of vacation

If for example, you want a 10 percent raise and have tried unsuccessfully every maneuver you know of to get it, you could go back to the list of options you prepared. Now might be a good time to propose a different solution, one that would still satisfy you. Working your way through your sets of options, you might suggest, for example, an 8 percent raise and tuition reimbursement for a $1,000 course instead of your original request of a 10 percent raise. Options are particularly important because we often don't know when there's a surplus of money in one area as compared to another. The professional development and training budget may have more means than the salary budget but we won't ever learn that unless we ask. Yet another option may involve less money but more vacation time. Propose an alternate solution, one that still satisfies your needs, in case your first option doesn't work out.

Ask yourself what is most important to you, where you want to remain firm, and what means less to you in a given asking situation. Then catalog your sets of options in order, just like the previous table illustrates. Bring it into your negotiation meeting and refer to it as needed. In addition, consider what negotiating experts refer to as a BATNA, or best alternative to a negotiated agreement. If the negotiation conversation reaches an impasse, what then? Will you leave the company, launch an external job search, or look for positions in other departments? Being careful not to concede too much—and yet giving yourself a range of alternatives—can be an incredibly freeing experience in a negotiation, not a constraining one.

PRACTICE OR PERISH!

This chapter has offered up several ways to help you get ready for a negotiation. Yet one tried-and-true piece of advice still applies: practice makes perfect. At a time when so much data are available to us, we should never ever go into a negotiating situation blindly winging it. April Carty-Sipp implores, "Practice and rehearse often! The more you do that, the more likely the outcome will be in your favor. If you don't take the time to rehearse or prepare, you have to ask yourself how much you really care about whatever it is you're negotiating for."

April's point completely resonates. If you won't prepare, are you really that deeply interested and invested in the outcome? Practice can occur in your car on the way to work speaking aloud to yourself, by jotting down a script of key points on paper, and certainly by hashing out the conversation with someone you trust. If you want to pinpoint exactly where you shine and need help, you can even record yourself rehearsing on a video camera or in front of a mirror. The important piece isn't how you do it, it's that you take the time to stack the deck in your favor by reviewing and repeating your arguments.

Often the better we know the facts of our case, the more we're willing to stay in the conflict until a truly two-way, beneficial outcome is reached. Preparing thoughtfully and rigorously through practice will help you keep your head, look smart, and give you an extra driving force when you're being disputed. Preparation is indeed your best friend in a negotiation.

5

Maneuvering Through
the Conversation

Your argument is clear. The background research on your counterpart is complete. Mentally, you are flying high. Does any of
this really matter once you're in the room on game day?

Extreme mountain climbing guides stress one key point with
their clients about the ascent up a rugged mountain: safety lies in
careful preparation. By contrast, inexperienced, and often younger,
climbers will explain that success boils down to game day: one's
step-by-step performance during the actual ascent and descent of
the mountain. We see a similar pattern when a home is being built.
An architect drafts minutely detailed plans, upholding that careful
planning and precision is the main way to realize success. Yet builders
see things differently, believing that actually erecting the building,
stacking each brick, is where true success or failure lies. The truth is,
both camps are right. And the same idea applies to negotiation.

We've established that preparation will give you more power
in a negotiation. Many tactics exist for boosting confidence, saving
face, and buying yourself time while in the heat of a discussion.
This chapter will give you a whole boxful of maneuvers, tactics, and
tools to help you navigate the conversation, from creating rapport
to the strategic use of silence. Some of these negotiating moves can
be counterintuitive at first and will require experimentation and

practice. Yet they will give you more agility and room for movement in a negotiation, and most important, they will give you options. Familiarity with making moves also gives you this essential edge: you'll recognize when they're being used on you!

UNDERSTAND THE ARCHITECTURE OF DEAL MAKING

You should always be able to commence a negotiation by setting a constructive tone. In Chapter Four, I showed how the structure of your ask conversation can be configured in an easy-to-follow, repeatable way. This structure assumes you will play an active role in the negotiation, not a supporting one in which you are led by the hand through the meeting. If you find yourself in a supporting role, watch for the way each of these steps plays out: paying attention to how the structure works, what it can look like, what happens when it breaks down—this is all valuable game-day experience in itself.

- *Tee up:* "This is what I'd like to discuss today . . . "
- *Ask:* "This is what I'm asking for . . . "
- *Substantiate:* "This is the rationale behind my case . . . "
- *Deepen:* "Tell me how you arrived at that conclusion . . . "
- *Appreciate and follow up:* "Thanks for sitting down with me to discuss this. I will plan to follow up with you next Tuesday as we discussed."

Because a negotiation is a volley or exchange of points, you may not need to call on all of these points in every situation or in the exact order presented. For example, you might be fortunate enough to get to step two—the ask—and find that your counterpart responds right away with a positive answer, eliminating the need for further negotiating (though not the need for follow-up). Similarly, you might enter a larger, more complicated deal in which you need to weave your ask and your substantiating research together. Regardless of the context, use your go-to architecture dynamically and it will give you a sense of ease and comfort in the large majority of your negotiating dialogues.

OPEN THE CONVERSATION ASSERTIVELY

The idea of who should speak first in a negotiation, and the bearing that has on favorability, has been hotly contested. Some say there is power in silence, in letting the other person speak first, because the onus is on the initiator to set a baseline for the match. There's also hope, among proponents of this method, that one's counterpart will reveal something previously unknown, perhaps something helpful to your side, by doing the talking first.

Others believe that you have more control if you kick off the negotiation, anchoring the discussion with an assertive figure or opening stake. Susan McFarland, executive vice president and principal accounting officer at Capital One, suggests, "Sometimes we're afraid to lay our hand on the table. But I don't leave a lot to chance on where I stand. Normally the better strategy is to make the first offer. Too often women think if they sit back and take it all in, listening before acting, they might get a better deal. Research shows, though, that we come out better if we make the first offer. You can't be clueless, mind you, you *must* know your stuff."

An anchor is named such because it's an opening metric that grounds and positions the rest of the deal. A classic example of this is in a car sale: a car is listed for sale at $30,000, so all subsequent negotiations tend to derive from that figure. A seller may think, "I'll list the car at $30,000 but I'll be happy if I get $28,000," whereas a buyer decides, "I will make an offer of $27,000, $3,000 less, because it's common to offer 10 percent less than the asking price." Regardless of the amount of an anchor, much of a deal's terms will emanate from it and we are usually influenced by it. For example, researchers Greg Northcraft and Margaret Neale had real estate agents evaluate a house, estimating its appraisal value and purchase price. Northcraft and Neale provided study participants with both high and low anchors representing the house's list price. Although each of the agents' estimates were influenced by the list price, they denied factoring the list price into their decisions, justifying their estimates with different features of the homes.[1]

As an active, equal participant in a negotiation, I encourage you to subscribe to the style of starting with an assertive opening number or request. If what you're buying is negotiable in price, only offer two-thirds to three-quarters of what you're willing to pay for something (depending on the product). Similarly, when stating your salary goals, set your figure high enough that you have room to work down. Adam D. Galinsky, an assistant professor at Northwestern University's Kellogg Graduate School of Management, has done research on exactly this aspect of deal making. Galinsky found that most negotiators make wimpy first offers, a propensity that's related to one's confidence and sense of control at the bargaining table.

What's an Aggressive Offer?

Your first offer should be the most aggressive you can make and still justify. In other words, an aggressive offer, if you were to get it, would thrill and delight you. Even though you're aiming high, you can still present an explanation and substantiation for the amount. You should always start here in a negotiation.

Galinsky has found that "many negotiators fear that an aggressive first offer will scare or annoy the other side and perhaps even cause [your counterpart] to walk away in disgust. However, research shows that this fear is typically exaggerated. In fact, most negotiators make first offers that are not aggressive enough."[2] Whenever you have the opportunity to make the opening offer, do so. Your assertive, ambitious anchor will drive the rest of the deal in your favor more than you realize.

Similarly, in your career, you will likely hear an initial offer that you like just as it is. Whether it's from a vendor, a supplier, a client, or a prospective employer, you may find that the other side has satisfied your interests, or at least the majority of them. The advice on accepting first offers is simple: don't do it! By coming to the bargaining table at all, a person is usually willing to negotiate *something*. For example, if a supplier opens a negotiation by offering your firm a 10 percent discount on their product's list price, you may be pleased. Perhaps you were ready to pay the list price. Still, the best approach is to negotiate for something else such as a favorable delivery cycle, customer service agreement, or other provision.

SET THE PACE

Often as we make an ask, the very last thing we're thinking about is pace. Yet, the best negotiators in the world take an active role in shaping a conversation's cadence. Ideally, you'll make your ask *progressively,* exposing more and more of the research you've done in a gradual manner. Why is this slow peeling of the onion important? Because in a negotiation, knowledge is power and you don't need to show your entire hand all at once.

Let's say you are negotiating with a vendor to lower the cost of its software. You may have three critical forces underpinning your ask: (1) you know of a competing vendor with better costs, (2) you're under a lot of pressure to cut the costs of the provider by 5 percent, and (3) you'd prefer to stick with this vendor at a lower rate than to go with a new vendor, based on the time investment to find and get the new vendor up to speed. Call on your strongest piece of evidence (which is often the least controversial or revealing about your situation) first. By discussing competitive rates, for example, you may find that you get a conciliatory reaction off the bat. A buyer's natural advantage is to compare prices and pick the best deal. Sure, you may have prepared more than that, but why use it if you don't have to? Be judicious with what you lay on the table, including how quickly you do it.

Putting a key reasoning out there and then allowing ample time for the dialogue volley helps you maintain power in the conversation. You are deciding what to reveal when—if it's even needed—and giving your counterpart time to digest each point. Also realize that often there's a data point that increases our vulnerability or exposure in a conversation. For example, sharing our deepest preferences or the upsetting pressures we're under can give the other side leverage. These are some of the reasons why we don't want to share, "I'll be crushed if I don't get this raise" or "I really need you to say 'yes' to my request of lowering your fees because I don't have the time or energy to find a replacement."

The message here is an important one. Knowledge and preparation give you a huge advantage but there's an art to unloading that information and weaving it into dialogue. Peel the onion back, layer by layer, as you exchange views, calling only on what you need, when you need it.

THINK CO-INVESTMENT

Negotiating with an eye for more isn't done just for the sake of pure greed. Whittling away at a deal until its terms improve is a natural "dance" in a negotiation. "One of the best predictors of negotiator satisfaction with an outcome is the number and size of the concessions extracted from an opponent. By making an aggressive first offer and giving your opponent the opportunity to 'extract' concessions from you, you'll not only get a better outcome, but you'll also increase the other side's satisfaction," says Adam Galinsky.[3] Be willing to make assertive claims but be equally comfortable giving up or adding on provisions that sweeten the deal for the other side. (To do this, of course, it's essential that you have determined what's most important for you to come out of the negotiation with and what you have the authority to decide concerning concessions.)

For example, an apparel company is not happy with the figure a consulting firm quotes them for some upcoming employee training work. For $20,000, the consulting firm will create a custom curriculum for the apparel company's two hundred employees. The consulting firm doesn't want to budge on its $20,000 price tag even when the client company pushes back on the figure. Rather than lowering their rate, the consultants attempt to incentivize the client with free additions that sound generous, but are actually low cost and low effort to the firm. By the firm throwing in two one-hour follow-up webinars, to reinforce the training curriculum among participants, the client feels it is getting a lot for its money. The consultants, however, don't have to use their most expensive trainer for the webinars and won't incur travel costs or excessive preparation time. The deal is accepted and both parties are satisfied. The consultants still get $20,000 and the client feels it has negotiated bonus offerings that make the price tag fairer.

Before lowering your ideal position in a negotiation, a helpful rule to remember is to give something away or add something to the pot that is of low importance to you. Imagine an employer is courting you and asking for your salary requirement. You say $90,000, knowing that you would be satisfied with $83,000. The employer balks at your figure, saying that although they like you, that number is a little high. Rather than do what can feel natural, which is to acquiesce and lower your number, consider a less intuitive move, which is upholding your figure, but offering something new to the mix. This is especially effective if you know what is particularly important to the other side. You might say, "Well, I'd prefer to stay with the $90,000 figure, but I am happy to move my start date earlier or to come in pro bono for a few days to train with my predecessor."

This approach takes a little practice, but its effectiveness at helping you hold on to what's important is unmatched. You come across as willing to flex and bend, yet you remain assertive and firm where it matters most.

COURT YOUR COUNTERPART

Negotiations are seriously helped by one element that lubricates the agreement: trust. Creating a rapport with someone, which can build trust, gives us a connection with the other party and helps to humanize our counterpart. For example, you build goodwill by saying, "I'm confident that we can find a mutually beneficial solution today...." You'll notice that the use of *we* can put your counterpart right at ease. Reinforcing a team approach with *we* and *us* language strengthens the likelihood of meeting your goal. Now *we* have a problem we're all trying to solve conjointly.

Let's assume you and a counterpart are waiting for a third negotiating party to enter the room. Being warm and approachable, you ask how your counterpart's weekend was. Your counterpart tells you he spent the weekend visiting universities with his college-bound teenager. The savviest negotiators will use this information to forge a deeper connection and find common ground. Exactly what you say in response isn't important but continuing to connect and dialogue with the other person, blending in your own experiences or

On Using Humor

"I was about twenty-four years old and prosecuting a rape case before an all-male jury in Kansas City, Missouri. My opponent was an older (so I thought at the time) and well-respected criminal defense attorney. It so happened that I was on a roll and scoring points with the jury during my cross-examining of his client, the defendant. In an apparent attempt to interrupt the momentum, he objected and said, 'Honey, would you approach the bench?' My immediate instinct, of course, was to take offense to being called 'honey' as a young female lawyer in the midst of a jury trial. As I was about to react, it dawned on me that the all-male jury would not likely feel my pain. So, I thought for a second, and replied 'Turtledove, I'll be right there.' The judge and jury could not hold back their laughter—and this defense attorney never called me 'honey' again. Knowing your audience and injecting humor in tense situations can often win the day."

—Carol Ann Petren, executive vice president and general counsel, MacAndrews & Forbes Holdings Inc.

similarities when possible, works. Sheila Murphy, associate general counsel at MetLife, suggests, "If I can, at the beginning, I try to diffuse tension. I make small talk and joke to get the relationship going. I always try to build rapport." Sheila continued, "To the extent you can, use humor to diffuse the situation. Don't come off as a hatchet. Soften your image where you can, drawing on good old PR methods." Being approachable can make your counterpart feel that negotiating with you is a pleasure, not a pain.

Marie Chandoha, president and CEO, Charles Schwab Investment Management, starts negotiations similarly. "I've spent lots of time observing men and women. Women can come to negotiations almost too serious in demeanor. A woman will often get right to the point, where men tend to infuse more humor and be more relaxed." Levity and, conversely, anxiety are contagious. We tend to spread them around, passing them off from one person to another on contact. Realize that fact in a negotiation and you'll find that adding some levity, humor, or humanity from the outset changes the dynamic of what's to follow. Irene Chang Britt, chief strategy officer at Campbell Soup Company, admits, "I've been told that I can be intimidating. I'm happy-go-lucky and joking personally, but I'm quite intense when it comes to business issues. How you carry yourself and the approach you take in a negotiation can be as meaningful as your content." To be sure, a negotiation can be driven from the opening tone and rapport created between parties. Why not make it as affable and comfortable as possible?

ESTABLISH YOUR CREDIBILITY

If we don't have credibility, we don't have much. The boy who cried wolf would probably agree. Credibility can be a tricky thing in a negotiation. Sometimes we have lots of it, through our performance, tenure, experience, or results. At other times, it feels like we have none. We may not know the other side or we may be coming at a negotiation with contentious, angry feelings. Sometimes we think the other side doesn't know what they're talking about and, horror of horrors, sometimes they think the same of us.

Whether or not this is the case, it can be helpful to weave in your credentials or knowledge in ways that are hard for the other side to argue with. Barbara J. Krumsiek, president, CEO, and chair of Calvert Investments, Inc., advises, "I think it's important for women to respect their résumés. I will try to weave into a conversation that I have math degrees or that I served on a national development team, for example. You might relate an anecdote that demonstrates your competence, without fully name-dropping. This is something we need to do skillfully; it's not merely reciting our credentials and it's not bragging either."

You can call on this tactic as needed in a negotiation, particularly if you feel your credibility is being called to question. There's no need to deliver a credibility booster in a haughty or defensive way; you can merely speak assuredly and factually, as the following examples show:

- Degrees or subject matter expertise
  - *Example:* "I can assure you I've reviewed the numbers carefully. I have two degree in math, which has helped me look at these calculations several different ways."
  - *Example:* "I've been negotiating terms like these for the past five years. I haven't seen vendors throw in a new complication like this at the last minute."
- Experiences you've had or observations you've made
  - *Example:* "When I was at ABC Company, we brokered deals like this all the time and I didn't face resistance on delivery terms."
  - *Example:* "It's hard to believe that none of your other clients demand better customer service availability from your firm when I know they operate in 24/7 environments."

As I noted previously, it's harder to refute someone's professional experience or the knowledge they've built up over a long period than, say, a gut feeling or whim they may have. Use that fact to your benefit and weave in, when needed, reminders of your credibility and expertise. This art can also be used in group negotiations, where you can substantiate credibility for someone else, perhaps touting a peer's expertise or experience in a given area.

ANTICIPATE PUSHBACK

We talked about anticipating objections in Chapter Four, but just how do we do this on the day of our big negotiation? Sheila Murphy advises, "If I know what their pushback is, I'll try to surface it in my opening remarks. I want to show them that I've stood in their shoes and looked at things from their perspective. This is especially important when there's emotion involved like with an employee decision." Beating others to the punch shows you're a thoughtful, big-picture thinker. It also shows you've critically looked at your idea or stance. Barbara J. Krumsiek recommends a proactive approach to pushback as well, noting, "I always address objections before they're raised. Sometimes I say, 'You might be wondering whether X could happen. . . . '"

Still, several possibilities exist for quelling disagreement. Susan McFarland offers, "When I was younger, I would enter a debate and hit home twenty-eight reasons why I was right, but I didn't look at what was important to the person across the table. Now I ask, 'Where can I create common ground?' I begin the debate with that common ground, and later I might go slightly left when they want to go right. Start with agreement, *then* move into areas of disagreement. Encourage cooperation and know your limits."

You can also mitigate objections by getting everyone into a team mentality. In a team environment, speaking your mind is encouraged and met receptively. "I give people the benefit of the doubt—assuming we all want the best outcome in a given situation," recalls Liz Lange, founder and creative director of Liz Lange Maternity. "I look at the people involved in a negotiation and behave as though we're all on the same side." This kind of conciliatory approach, rather than an adversarial one, can get counterparts in the mind-set of solving an overarching problem or mitigating a risk that everyone's facing and that everyone needs to solve.

BE A RELENTLESS PROBLEM SOLVER

One of the best roles you can assume in a negotiation is that of the relentless problem solver. Not quick to give in, you maneuver in such a way that you're respectful of the person but tough on the problem. Even still, there may be moments when someone else's agenda threatens to overtake your negotiation. Lori A. Greenawalt, partner at KPMG LLP, notes, "Don't let anyone derail you! In the really tough conversations, this can be hard to avoid. But go back to your intent and don't let the conversation get too tangential. If someone is derailing the conversation, say, 'That's important, but not for today's conversation. We can address that another day.'"

As any good problem solver knows, by bending a little, you can engender just the kind of cooperation to get a deal done. Use validating language when you're getting pushback, not just because it shows respect for the other side, but also because you may be hearing something you didn't factor in. You might respond to a point or piece of pushback by saying, "Your point is one I hadn't heard until now and it gives me a better sense of your department's needs; however, ... " Often in a negotiation, people repeat their points because they don't feel heard. The tactic of validating others' pushback can be especially powerful in helping someone to feel heard and understood. It's also important in minding your language, to avoid using *never* and *always,* terms that convey rigidity and an unwillingness to move from one's position.

Still, getting pushback on our ideas can easily suck away our optimism and leave us feeling deflated. How will you manage in the face of pushback? Liz Lange recollects, "There have certainly been times when I didn't get support or I had to prove something to persuade advisors and boards. If my counterparts are skeptical, I make a point to stay enthusiastic." By showing that your belief and commitment are unflinching, others will more easily get on board with your ideas.

Furthermore, surfacing issues and getting everyone working on the problems can get you just the kind of cooperation you're looking for.

APPEAL TO THEIR SENSE OF FAIRNESS

Certainly, we can't walk into negotiations assuming everyone has the same moral compass. Yet, a kind of persuasion exists that calls on a sense of universal rights and wrongs. Chester L. Karrass, a researcher and famed negotiation trainer, offers up one way to do this. "Just say to them, 'Put yourself in my shoes.' You will be pleasantly surprised at how often the shoes fit."[4] The level of fairness in a deal is a major driver in overall satisfaction. When you ask for a fair arrangement rather than one that's perfectly suited to you, counterparts tend to be more generous.

Another way to get to a fairer deal is to use the time-tested gem, "Is that the best you can do?" You can also refine this question to be more open-ended, asking, "Can you do any better?" When asked such direct questions, our instinct is often to try a little harder to help the other side.

Whether there's a lack of fairness in the process of the negotiation or the outcome itself, don't be afraid to surface the issue. Appealing to your counterpart's ethics in this manner is one more way of ensuring you get an equitable result, by not backing down or agreeing to less-than-ideal terms too quickly.

APPEAL TO A HIGHER POWER

There are times when we have no choice but to follow a certain chain of command when negotiating. One example of this is that you ask your boss, rather than your boss's boss, for a raise. We show respect by going to the immediate authority on a matter, proceeding up the chain hierarchically as needed. The problem is that being respectful can get us stuck at the negotiating table with someone who isn't empowered to help us.

Salespeople don't bother to pitch their product to non–decision makers and neither should you. In fact, seasoned sales professionals spend a lot of their time before a negotiation ever happens making sure that they are selling to the true authority. When faced with a choice of whom to include in a negotiation, simply ask yourself, "Is everyone I'm inviting empowered to make a decision?" At a bare minimum, the individuals should be able to go back to their managers and advocate for a point of view one way or another, even if they don't have ultimate say.

It's important to be vigilant against encounters in which you are negotiating with someone only to have them pass the buck at the last minute. You may be bargaining over the specifications of a work order when you're told at the eleventh hour, "I'll have to check with my management team on whether that's possible." On occasion, that might be fine with you, but when pressed for time, you may need an answer sooner. You can respond by saying, "I've been under the impression all along that you had authority to decide on this matter. If I've been wrong about that, then I'm not sure it makes sense for us to continue to negotiate."

Although your counterpart may have a genuine need to consult others, sometimes you'll be put in this situation when your counterpart is engaging in a power play. Perhaps you're being firm or stubborn on a given point and the other side wants to test how willing you are to really find common ground. Whatever the case, it's important to be resolute but reasonable if someone isn't fully authorized to call the shots.

SAY IT LIKE THEY'D SAY IT

The way you deliver your messages has an essential bearing on how they'll be received. The best way to package our messages is to consider how our counterpart speaks and operates. As a perennial rule, we must avoid qualifying our ideas with caveats such as, "This might be a silly idea … " or "I'm not an expert but … " When we use such phrasing, we instantly erode our credibility and convey our own uncertainty about what we're offering up. I'd argue that we actually hurt our standing by qualifying our ideas in this way, essentially professing to others, "Don't give much credence to what I'm about to say, it's pretty half baked."

Assuming you've done your homework on how your counterpart communicates and which dominant style he or she tends to favor, use mimicry to make your idea shine. "I know the importance of finding the right way and time to deliver something," says Darlene Slaughter, VP, chief diversity officer at Fannie Mae. "I make a case in my counterparts' *own* language when presenting something. I use words that sound much like their own, so it feels like they said it."

What about when we need to communicate that we're similar and yet remain firm on an issue? "It's possible to be both assertive and respectful. You don't have to be edgy. Find a happy balance … ," suggests Karen Ganzlin, chief human resources officer at TD Ameritrade. Mirroring another's style isn't about being inauthentic as a person. It's about flexing to the audience at hand and tailoring your style to best meet their needs. Speak like your counterpart speaks and many times you'll watch resistance melt.

Packaging your message smartly and directly will win you respect and influence in a negotiation. As we discussed in Chapter Four, careful preparation means taking the time to learn *their* way of communicating. Then on game day your content can shine and you can woo your audience. Linda Descano, president and CEO of

Women & Co., a program of Citibank, advises, "Sometimes we use acronyms and assume others know what we mean. And yet, they don't have the same reference points as we do. Be certain that your style, story, and even analogies are relevant. Recently my staff came back from a training and they were irritated that every analogy used to teach was golf related. This alienated the audience and they also didn't walk away with the key points. You can't influence if you don't speak the audience's language." Cautionary tales like Linda's abound. Don't let yourself become one of them!

CALL ON YOUR CONVICTION

As you ready yourself to sink your teeth into the meaty issues of a negotiation, you'll be helped by considering one particular aspect of your pitch. You must convey your point with passion. The truth is, if you can't offer your point compellingly, like it really matters, then you probably shouldn't be making a pitch in the first place.

Deborah Simpson, chief financial officer of The Boston Consulting Group, advises, "Show some passion for what you're trying to sell. Find the right blend between conviction and belief in your recommendation and getting overly attached emotionally to the outcome." April Carty-Sipp, SVP of creative services, Comcast Sports Group, agrees: "Being passionate is the most important part of being persuasive. If you really believe in something, others can sense it. Don't be afraid to show your fervor or be animated." Indeed, if you have not bought into your own idea, why should others buy into it? Enthusiasm is a good thing in negotiation; use it to convey your creativity and commitment to a positive outcome.

The art of persuasion requires a balancing act between showing genuine conviction and letting go of the ending outcome. Rebecca Baker, chief marketing officer and global partner, Alvarez & Marsal, agrees. "It's essential to convey your passion and belief in your cause without pushing people in a particular way. This has very much been a learned skill for me. Historically, if I had a good idea, I became so committed to it that I'd present it as 'the only way.' What I've learned is that the cooler I can be—even if there's volcanic activity below the surface—the better I can answer questions coming at me."

Communicating your points fervently demonstrates the foundational belief that you have bought into your own idea. Then it demonstrates that others should, too. Being genuinely enthusiastic about a request or concept also makes it harder for people to reject your concept or say no. "If we're too assertive, we can cross over to being called the 'B' word. Once you're labeled like that, it's hard to change people's minds. I try to stop short of that. There's a better way to make your point.... You need to paint a clear picture of how a change will be better for the company, by either creating a common goal or showing how failure is the common enemy. You need to exude care and show people what *could be,*" advises Irene Chang Britt. Indeed, caring and passion for your vision can lubricate your creakiest negotiation.

EXERCISE SILENCE

Being quiet seems like the very last thing we should do in a negotiation. For women, who in particular can be perceived as more passive than men, surely a tacit approach is not the best one, right? Contrary as it may seem, I strongly encourage you to embrace and leverage silence. Being quiet in actuality is a negotiation must. You'll find that in doing so, several options open up:

- Your counterpart may perceive a leveling of the power.
- Your counterpart will often feel a need to fill the silence or finish your sentence.
- Your counterpart may expose a piece of information that you didn't know but needed.

- You have more time to collect your thoughts, processing what you just heard.
- You have more time to consider your next step, including a change in course.
- Silence may show that you are engaged; you're carefully considering your counterpart's view or deliberating on a point.

Strategically using silence means that you go slowly, pausing and leaving gaps throughout the conversation. It doesn't just come in handy after you say something but is a tactic you can use in between conversation points and exchanges. Simply put, silence's effect on others can put you in a more favorable position. The use of silence becomes most important at two critical junctures in a negotiation. The first is right after you make a request. The second is right after your counterpart answers. When you tell a client, for example, that you can offer them five hundred products at a cost of $1,000 each—of course, your best price—your safest move is to deliver that ask cleanly and clearly. This means you don't hesitate afterward and begin adding words to lessen your request or soften the blow. You also don't want to qualify your ask by saying something like, "if you can afford it" or "I know this has been a rough year for the company." Give yourself instead at least seven seconds of silence to let your ask sink in and to show that you stand behind it.

When your counterpart comes back to you with a response, whether a counterargument or agreement, be sure to again engage in silence. Let's say you ask your manager for his blessing for you to serve as the head of a new internal committee. He responds by telling you that your workload is likely to increase and therefore he doesn't want you to be overcommitted or saddled with distractions. Sitting quietly, you listen to his explanation, careful not to nod your head as though you're in agreement, but keeping a neutral facial expression. Again, give yourself seven seconds to be silent. This maneuver will often push your counterpart to explain their reasoning, sometimes even causing him or her to back out of it and come up with a different response altogether.

Seeing the value in silence also means recognizing when it's being used on you. Often we negotiate against ourselves when we give something away or jump in with a concession just because the other side is quiet. After all, the counterpart may be pondering the deal, having zero disagreement with our stance, yet we may let his or her silence drive our actions! You can handle a quiet period by being quiet yourself or asking deepening questions such as, "What do you think about the terms of the deal?" You can equip yourself with a handy tool such as a file or your notes if you want to look away and give the other side some time. You can also breathe your way through silence, resisting the very natural urge to pipe up and fill the air. When you engage in a negotiation, keep the following points in mind and remember to put a cushion of silence around each step:

- Say your piece . . .
- Wait and breathe . . .
- Let the other person think . . .
- Let the other person speak . . .
- Before replying, pause . . .
- Then reply . . .
- Leave space for the other person to concede something, move toward your side, or to answer his or her own question.

The next time you're in a negotiation situation, experiment with being quiet rather than speaking up right away or thanking your counterpart. Although it can feel awkward at first, silence lobs the ball into the other person's court, often resulting in your counterpart giving you a surplus of information. As women, we need to use silence to our advantage even if our conditioning leads us to want to accommodate others, be conciliatory, or worry that we're being difficult. Indeed, silence, when well used, is a great leveler of power and one of your trustiest friends!

Use Your Body

Sometimes an added bit of body language can augment your use of silence. A smile, even a shrug, can convey worlds of information. Body language can also do quite the opposite, impregnating silence with a clue but not an absolute stance one way or another. The best negotiations occur when participants keep their bodies open and receptive to input. This means being inclusive of all members of a negotiation, making sure that you turn to look, listen, and speak to all members.

Many of us learn best how to carry ourselves by reflecting on our habits or behavior in a meeting. Fizzah Jafri, COO, Fixed Income Research and Economics at Morgan Stanley, notes, "Both my husband and my boss have told me that when I am defending a point or making a case, I always sit back and fold my arms. You don't need to be a body language expert to know that that's seen as defensive. Now I go out of my way to leave my arms at my sides or to talk animatedly with them. I use my body to show that I'm listening by writing down people's points or keeping my body open. It's important to smile, relax, and be approachable—to look comfortable in your skin." Fizzah went on to explain a phenomenon she sees in other women: sometimes we can make out bodies smaller, almost crouching when we're nervous. And yet, the last thing we want to do is minimize ourselves.

How can you know the best course of action for using your body? The best policy is openness and authenticity. If you're shocked or surprised by an announcement, it's okay to be real and show that amazement with a slight flinch. If you're baffled, you might scratch your head. If you're encouraged, you might smile. Regardless of what you do, find your own power in being quiet and using your body at times, and you will improve your negotiation skills by leaps and bounds.

Catherine Ann Mohan, partner and treasurer at McCarter & English, recognizes that the tenor and volume of her voice helped her establish credibility. "First impressions for women are so significant. If you want to persuade others, you'd better stand up, say your name, and make your case without apologizing for it. I have a very strong voice; I've never been told I'm soft spoken. I believe that kind of detail matters. When I walk into a room and have done my homework and am confident in my opinion, it influences others. The confidence, and even the volume with which you speak, shows others how much you believe in yourself." Contrasting this viewpoint, Rosemary Turner, president of Chesapeake UPS, notes, "I'm direct. People know where I stand on issues.... If there's something especially important I need to say—where I really need to be heard—I'll sometimes lower my voice. My team will tell you they know it's time to listen when I do that." If you want to create a less adversarial feeling in a negotiation, consider sitting side by side when it makes sense as opposed to face to face. By keeping your torso open and your posture tall, you can more easily speak with a credible pitch and volume. After all, you need to say it like you mean it. Finally, maintaining confident, direct eye contact can say volumes about your level of engagement and focus on the discussion at hand.

Do you slouch, frown, look down, or shout when you make a case? If you want to know the answer, consider seeing yourself on video. You could be giving a presentation, making a sales pitch, or leading a meeting. Whatever the situation, have it recorded and go back and watch yourself with a compassionate, constructive eye. You will gain critical, needed feedback about how you use your body when making a case. This kind of data can be so eye-opening; in fact, it can help you refine your physical behavior immediately.

REACH FOR EXPANSIVE, DEEPENING QUESTIONING

Beyond using silence strategically, you can empower yourself by getting proficient at expansive questioning. These are questions that open up dialogue, getting to deeper issues than those on the surface. They give you more information about your counterpart and show your interest in understanding your counterpart's realities.

Dead-end questioning, however, tends to invite curt, surface-level answers. Often asked in a reactionary way, these questions force a "yes" or "no" answer or a defensive response, and they can narrow or polarize a negotiation. Deepening questions, some examples of which are shown in the following list, help guide and move the conversation along, making a mutually beneficial result much more likely.

Deepening Questions
- Can you explain how you arrived at that solution?
- Can you walk me through how decisions like these are determined?
- What do you think is keeping us from coming to an agreement?
- How could I help you feel more comfortable with this request?
- What is the best way for us to . . . ?
- How willing are you to negotiate that point?
- What is most important to you? Can you explain why?
- How can we move forward?
- How can we best . . . ?
- How can we both win?
- How can we make this work for both of us?
- Is that the best you can do? Can you say more about why that's the case?

- Can you help me understand what you are trying to satisfy or accomplish?
- What is the cost of us not coming to an agreement?

Here are some examples of the difference between closed and open questioning in common asking situations. Note how combative the dead-end questioning can come across.

Dead-End Questioning	Expansive Questioning
So you think I only deserve a 3 percent raise?	Can you explain how you arrived at that raise percentage? Tell me about your thinking.
Why is the price fixed?	Can you elaborate on your rationale for using fixed pricing? I'd like to get a better sense of where you're coming from.
Why aren't you willing to negotiate the delivery terms?	Can you help me understand what's constraining you with the delivery terms?

Strengthen your own appeal by asking good questions. Like silence, questioning is a safe place to be, favorable in that you are collecting more information rather than giving anything way or agreeing too quickly to terms you'll later regret. Asking questions can get you needed information, buy you more time to think, and help you get to the heart of what is upsetting your counterpart. These queries can yield "negotiation gold" in the sense that you can learn exactly what is on your counterpart's mind, helping you reshape your message or change directions.

CALLING ON DELAYS

More often than not, there are pressures in timing to get a deal done or come to a negotiated agreement. This is all well and good in moving a conversation forward, except when you're uncomfortable with the terms. Our discomfort can come from being less familiar than we'd like with the subject matter, needing more time to think something through or needing to involve someone not at the negotiating table. Sheila Murphy admits, "I don't get locked into an answer if I don't have enough information. If pressed, I postpone giving an answer so that I can preserve my credibility. There's nothing wrong with saying, 'I'll think about that and get back to you.'"

I'm a firm believer that no one can show her leadership potential if she doesn't demonstrate that she can grapple with issues, rather than deferring them to someone else. Still, there is absolutely nothing wrong with taking breaks or moving to stop a negotiation. This is never more important than in a "drive-by" negotiation situation, in which you're surprised or spontaneously engaged in a matter.

"I like to be prepared to say, 'Let me get back to you on that,'" recalls Barbara J. Krumsiek. "I never let myself think that we must finish everything today. If you do that, you may inadvertently make a concession or shut a door too quickly." Indeed, if we let timing demands take too large a role, our own decision-making abilities may be tainted and weakened in the name of coming to an agreement. If you're forced into a short frame of time, let's say to consider a job offer, then negotiate to elongate the window. You don't have to agree to a time limit just because it's given to you.

What's more, if you don't have enough information about your counterpart to be a strong negotiator, consider rescheduling. DeeDee Wilson, SVP of finance at L.L.Bean, advises, "If I'm pitching to my boss for example, I really think about how he or she benefits by saying 'yes' to what I'm asking. Taking the time to really understand what matters to my constituents is well worth the investment." As women, we face an added complication here. Many of us worry that we'll be seen as difficult or as though we're asking for special accommodations if we call for a break or delay. My answer to those fears is that it's better to look difficult than to sign off on something you'll later regret. In fact, delays are often the saving grace that preserves our credibility just before we might erupt or do something we'll regret.

On Buying Time

"One time, my boss and I were in disagreement about some employee changes. We hadn't reached resolution on how the issue would affect one employee. Nonetheless, my boss spontaneously called the employee into a meeting of ours and firmly announced the change to the employee. I was angry. I wasn't in the right state of mind to handle the situation well. I didn't want to support a decision I disagreed with—but I didn't want to not support my boss either. I asked to leave the room. Then I got up and left, just like that. Needless to say, I didn't sleep well that night. I assumed that I had made a career-ending move. The next morning, though, I went into my boss's office and immediately he said, 'I'm sorry, I shouldn't have popped that on you. I didn't handle it well.' There's something to be said for removing yourself from a situation when you sense it'll end in disaster. Don't do something reactionary in the moment."

—Susan McFarland, executive vice president and principal accounting officer at Capital One

---

DE-ESCALATE DEADLOCKS

As long as human beings are the ones at the negotiating table, we can count on negotiations fluctuating—often unpredictably—in tone and dynamics. The great news is that if you sense a negotiation is getting derailed or becoming overly contentious, there are plenty of tactics to call on to lessen tension in a situation. "There's far more optionality than most people call upon in negotiations. Instead of 'no,' try saying 'How about ... ?'" says Susan McFarland.

Encountering deadlocks also present a good time to push aside whatever style hasn't been working and introduce a fresh new way. For example, you might say, "We seem to be running in circles here. Let's try something new." You can try an idea-generation technique (see the following), reschedule, or move to a new environment. You can also bring in new members to negotiate, invigorating the group with new perspectives. If all else fails, you may indeed need to leave the room without reaching agreement.

I encourage you to invent creative options when there aren't any. Don't be afraid to go to the whiteboard, for example, and plot out people's views in a chart, create a SWOT analysis, or otherwise facilitate a constructive way to move the conversation forward. Put on your facilitator hat and take some ownership for getting people unstuck. Here are some techniques for you to try; use your judgment to see if they will fit with your particular audience:

Brainwriting: All ideas are recorded by the individual who thought of them. They are then passed on to the next person who uses them as a trigger for his or her own ideas.

Brainstorming: This method generates fresh material by deferring judgment and encouraging and recording wild ideas. It can be done anonymously or openly, where ideas are attached to their inventors.

Visualization: Use mapping and drawing techniques to sketch out a problem using data, information, concepts, strategies, or metaphors. For example, you might sketch a complex problem out in a map, showing the terrain, mountains, valleys, and tricky passages of the initiative.

Trigger sessions: After a "problem owner" defines a problem, each group member writes down two ideas in two minutes. Participants read out their lists one by one, adding ideas inspired by others' concepts. Trigger sessions can continue for several passes until ideas literally run dry.

Numerous techniques exist for moving a conversation forward. You may need to let ideas percolate with a group, allowing ample time for analysis and discussion. If members of the group need to take a zigzag approach, for example, then let them. Susan McFarland notes, "One boss said to me, 'Susan, your problem is that you arrive so quickly at what we *ought* to do but others haven't gotten there. You argue hard to get everyone else there.' In geometry the shortest distance between two points is a straight line. But in business a straight line may not be the fastest way between two points. Bring others along by listening. Take what they say and connect it to your right course of action."

Another one of the handiest techniques you can use—and my personal favorite—is the 70/20/10 rule. When stuck in a conversation in which someone is resisting or pushing back unrelentingly, try allocating your time as follows:

- 70 percent of the time engage in active listening
- 20 percent of the time ask deepening or clarifying questions
- 10 percent of the time push your own agenda or try to change the other person's mind

When you experiment with this rule, you'll witness an amazing thing happen. Opposition often melts. Darlene Slaughter declares, "I don't ever want to walk out of a meeting with someone feeling damaged or like they've lost his or her dignity. I really listen. I factor in what I'm hearing. That approach will generally cause people to be at ease and back down. It's not necessary to dig your heels in." Those pushing back the hardest often want to be heard the most. By actively listening and through a level of mirroring and mimicry, you give the spotlight to your counterpart and his or her concerns, creating an environment in which escalation naturally lessens. When you experience the magic of really listening in a negotiation, you find that you're doing less of the talking and yet you become more powerful.

CONCEDING

One thing you can do is to consider making a concession—depending on the negotiation, only after you've tried all the other techniques presented here, and perhaps at an earlier point, for leverage. As discussed in Chapter Four, preparation should always involve knowing what you can and are willing to concede and, conversely, what you feel absolutely unyielding about. Then coming up with creative solutions and concessions is one more way to show your willingness to get to common ground in a negotiation. However, if you must concede something, you always want to be prepared to negotiate to get something else back so that you don't make accommodations unnecessarily.

Lucy S. Danziger, editor-in-chief of *SELF Magazine,* says, "There are certain things you know you can win and some you can't. When I negotiate with an outside vendor, for example, I might not be able to get a better price, but I can always find other areas where my company can get more benefit. I might ask for something free from my counterpart, like sharing website traffic or more time on a schedule." Getting 90 percent of what you want is indeed better than settling for 50 percent.

Conceding involves the delicate art of allowing the other person to save face and gain some power. It's where you show a level of empathy for your counterpart's situation or view. Put another way, be prepared to give something in order to get ahead. As you do so, remember that value is perceived. What may be a small gesture to you may appear significant to your counterpart. Start with the biggest small concession you're willing to make as a means to build some goodwill and then taper future concessions so that they're of minimal effort or injury to you. This conveys that you really worked with the other person and that they got a good deal.

Karen Ganzlin reinforced this idea by noting, "As one person, you'll never have all the answers. Often, someone might have thought of something you didn't. The more points of view, the better your decision will be. Be willing to say, 'That's a good point. I hadn't considered it.'" Concessions can come in the form of admitting the value of someone else's point or it can be more of a gesture or gift. Barbara Krumsiek emphasized this by noting, "One important element in style is generosity. This trait can be especially positive for women. Even though we might worry that we'll be taken advantage of, or appear soft, generosity can be the jet fuel that saves a difficult situation." By saying something like, "Tom, I can appreciate your concerns about the delivery date in question. I'm willing to move on that if you can offer me a better rate on the multiyear deal," you are giving and getting. The best way to make a concession is to offer one up while asking for a different one back. This maneuver calls on the principle of reciprocity, and it's ingratiating. When we're given something, most people feel compelled to give something back. Often this willingness to move from our original position, even if it's just a little, is what moves a negotiation out of stagnation.

"It is almost impossible to have worked as many years as I have without having been the lone voice on an issue. It's never easy. Still, you should leave at the door any thoughts of inflexibility in changing your position on issues," offers Carol Ann Petren.

Carol's point underscores an important research discovery. Previously we looked at research from Adam Galinsky that showed that one of the best predictors of negotiator satisfaction with an outcome is the number and size of the concessions extracted from an opponent. Satisfaction matters, according to Galinsky, because "a satisfied opponent will be more likely to live up to the terms of the agreement and less likely to seek future concessions or revenge."[5] By giving away something of low importance, you may just create the kind of negotiation relationships that can endure.

MANAGING BULLYING AND BELITTLING

Unfortunately, at some point, you will find yourself in a situation where someone attempts to "win" at negotiating by minimizing your point of view, your position, even you as a person. The hardest part about being the recipient of this tactic is that it's often effective at shutting us down, allowing the bully to override us completely.

I can remember clearly being in this type of uncomfortable situation. While at one of my first jobs out of school—a boutique consulting firm—I found myself desperately miserable. Among other qualities, the firm had a caustic atmosphere in which managers freely and consistently berated employees. I was starting to have physical, not just emotional, effects, and knew I needed to do something. I had trudged through the first six months of employment miserable yet hoping things would improve, but in the following three months they only got worse. Without another job lined up, I walked in one day and offered my resignation and explained why I was leaving. Among other logistics, the HR manager curtly informed me that my benefits would continue through the remainder of the month. One week later then, I thought nothing of visiting the dentist, yet was informed by my dentist that I wasn't covered by any insurance.

Calling my former boss to explain and remedy the situation was uncomfortable at best. The very last thing I wanted to do was ask for help from an entity I couldn't stand. "Selena," my former boss said, "You don't exactly have a lot of equity built up here. You left the firm after less than a year even though you said in your interview you were looking to make a longer term commitment. We're not exactly going to bend over backward to help."

That I was a nuisance, a burden, and a disappointment were all coming through loud and clear as we talked on the phone. Throughout our tense exchange, my confidence was eroding and I wondered if I had any business making this request in the first place. Still, on a deep level, and regardless of how I felt about the firm or my former boss, I knew that fair was fair. Shocking myself, I declared, "Scott, this arrangement wasn't what either of us expected. All I'm asking for here is something that I was promised." To my amazement, the firm soon took care of making sure their insurer paid the claim.

Realize that belittlers are often good at what they do. They are skilled at shaming, blaming, and devaluing others, actions that often make the recipients devalue themselves. The best remedy is to expect and prepare for such a reaction, having a game plan for what you'll do. Your action plan can be as simple as choosing to go back to your notes or key headlines rather than back down if you feel you're getting pushed around.

In the case of Fizzah Jafri, she likes to ask for specific illustrations of someone's objection. "If someone is going to contest your performance, you must ask for specific examples. Make people uncomfortable. Put the person on the spot and ask for very clear feedback. Ask, 'What exactly did I do wrong and what can I do to fix it?' If someone can't give you answers to those questions, there's a larger problem." Rather than simply acquiescing to a negative appraisal of you, your idea, or your work, insist on objective data. Push back.

In the face of heightened emotion, facts represent your best touchstone. Anticipate how you will stay composed, even while being tested, and remain firm. Most of all, realize that you have a place at the table and that there's value in your request.

CLOSE THE DEAL

One of the greatest mistakes we can make in a deal is assuming that because things are going well, closing more formally is not needed. Even if potential clients are giving us every encouraging cue that they want to move forward—nodding their head, smiling at our proposed terms, even giving us verbal affirmation—we can still lose out if we fail to close.

Closing involves clarifying and summarizing all that's been agreed on throughout the conversation. It also gives us a chance to get clear on and arrange for next steps. If we find that our counterpart wants to delay closing, we can use techniques to entice him or her to get the deal done now. Charles Karrass recommends asking the simple but powerful question, "If not now, when?"[6] This brilliant little question removes arbitrary time stamps and can halt someone else's delay strategy.

Another tactic suggests that you emphasize the downside of not reaching an agreement now. By explaining, for example, that not reaching agreeable terms means a project will be delayed even further than it already is, we can often get people on board with a decision. By contrast, you can explain—and even create—upsides to getting the deal done now. Find ways to sweeten the deal if an agreement is made today.

One more approach for closing deals is to minimize the work required of your counterpart. In Chapter Four, I advised you to do creative prework such as coming up with a sample telecommuting agreement when you're asking for that kind of work arrangement. By creating an outline that paints a bold picture and makes it easy for an individual to simply sign off, you make it one step closer to achieving clear agreement. Similarly, take initiative by offering to follow up a negotiation with a summary in writing. This protects both sides and wards against misunderstandings, which we'll talk about in more detail in Chapter Six.

When you want to close, follow a rational and fact-based approach. Present where you've been in the conversation, what agreement had been reached, and how any actions will proceed. Don't overlook continuing to build goodwill with your counterparts by emphasizing your appreciation of them and their willingness to negotiate and your confidence that the arrangement will be a positive one. Remember, take account of the recency effect to accentuate your most important points at the end of your presentation.

NEVER UNDERVALUE YOUR POWER

Wharton professor Richard Shell has done intriguing research into the most detrimental assumptions that we make in negotiations. His findings show three common types of faulty hypotheses:

- Assuming that a high level of conflict exists
- Assuming that everybody thinks the same way
- Overestimating the other party's power or underestimating your own power[7]

It is especially important as women not to underestimate our abilities. Given that our sense of self-agency hasn't often been emphasized (as it typically is with males), we may need to continually remind ourselves of our own authority. Remember that your counterpart wouldn't be negotiating with you if he or she didn't think you had some power in the first place. What's more, realize you aren't alone, stuck, or without the ability to try something new. In life, at work, and certainly in a negotiation, you always have options, a major source of power. Claim them and use them.

See and treat yourself as powerful—as the chief executive of your own life—and people will respond. You may not come out of each negotiation with the perfect arrangement but you will have the best kind of strength of all: a healthy sense of your own voice and power.

6

Follow Up

Ending a negotiating situation is a heady experience. We can walk away exhilarated, fatigued, frustrated, or relieved among myriad other reactions. We may be proud of getting up the gumption to go and ask for it or feel completely defeated, knowing we didn't push back enough. Regardless of how we walk away, there's usually at least some emotion attached to the experience.

The period immediately after a negotiation can be more important than it seems initially. We can easily assume that the true heavy lifting takes place in the preparation for and actual maneuvering through the negotiation. Yet the follow-up period after a negotiation can have a major bearing on our getting what we just negotiated for. Assuming we follow up proactively in writing, as I ardently recommend, we have a framework for future conversation and movement forward.

For a negotiation to be successful, both sides must feel that they can live with the agreed-on terms. The immediate aftermath of the negotiation can contribute to the feelings, positive or negative, that your counterpart has about your agreement, and the actions you take now can build trust—or do the opposite. Following up a negotiation in a structured way with your counterpart can keep your agreement and your relationship on track.

The period after a negotiation is also a valuable opportunity to assess and consolidate our skills. This is a kind of follow-up, too, and from the perspective of building our pushback skills, it's just as valuable as the preparation and game-day stages. We'll talk about this personal kind of follow-up first.

DO YOUR OWN POSTMORTEM

The very best place to start your postbargaining activities is by doing an assessment of the negotiation shortly after it's over. If you're feeling pretty neutral about the negotiation, you can do this immediately following it. If, however, you're very emotionally charged, then take some time, perhaps a day to clear the fog and start collecting your thoughts. Don't let more time than that pass, though, or your memories and perceptions won't be as sharp and complete and your learning won't be as strong.

Ask yourself the following questions:

- How did I feel during the negotiation? What about afterward?
- What words would I use to describe the kind of negotiator I was?
- What observations would a neutral third party make about the negotiation?
- How did my approach compare to the pushback credo in Chapter Two?
- Is there an approach or maneuver that I'd like to use next time?

In answering these questions without letting too much time pass, you'll get a great sense of where you excelled. You'll also surface the places where you could have been more effective, and you'll do so in a constructive, proactive way rather than a nagging, festering way.

A good postmortem gives you more power. You'll have nearly instant information on how to step up your game and leverage what you already do best. If someone else was negotiating on your side, you can also include that person in your self-assessment. Marie Chandoha, president and CEO of Charles Schwab Investment Management, says, "Self-analysis has been important to me, but having good advisors in my life has been even more important. There will always be some things you're not conscious of and advisors can help with this." You can call on your teammate to tell you two areas where you excelled and two instances where you can improve next time.

As you look back on your negotiation, and with the goal of trying to learn constructively and nonjudgmentally, try to nail down three moments or maneuvers you made that had the biggest impact, good or bad, on your performance. You can write them here or use another piece of paper.

List the three moments you had or maneuvers you made that had the biggest impact, good or bad, on how the conversation went.

1. _____

2. _____

3. _____

Now elaborate on these moments. Write out what you said, what you were thinking, and—if the moment went badly—another way you can approach the situation next time. You should also include where or how you were most effective in the conversation.

	What I Said or Did	What I Was Thinking	Another Way I Could Say or Do It	Where or When I Was Most Effective
Example	"I'll accept your job offer at a salary of $65,000."	"I'm still not satisfied with $65,000 but it's probably a bad idea to keep bargaining."	"I appreciate the movement you've made to get to $65,000 but I'd be more comfortable with a figure like $70,000. If you could meet me there, I could start in two weeks."	Rather than merely accept the $65,000 salary and job, I first asked for the rationale behind that figure.
1.				
2.				
3.				

INITIATE A FEEDBACK EXCHANGE

Self-analysis is important but so is feedback from others. Sometimes when we're filled to the brim with new self-knowledge and crystal clear on how the other person screwed up, we want to "educate" anyone who'll listen. Perhaps we want to impart what we've learned to the other side, opening their eyes to their dooming blind spots. This is a good idea if the negotiation has been respectful or cordial. It may prove to be an even better idea if your debate hasn't gone that amicably. "If someone really rubbed you the wrong way, tell them," offers Susan McFarland, executive vice president and principal accounting officer at Capital One. "They usually don't know they did it. If you keep letting it go, it will take overal.... Couch it as, 'I struggle with it when you do ... ' Be sure they understand it's your problem, not theirs. Most people get uncomfortable when you confront them in this way but it often leads to a behavior change." The feedback you give may be related to behaviors, outcomes, or the very processes used to negotiate.

What's more, we can't give feedback every time we converse with someone. Susan McFarland went on to say, "Be thoughtful. Don't tell everyone they hurt your feelings. Pick and choose the times and situations to surface issues or emotions." Remember that the primary use of feedback in the aftermath of a negotiation is to support the relationship and the agreement. Thus it should be honest but constructive.

Here are some good guidelines for delivering feedback:

- Ask them first. Beat your counterpart to the punch by asking if they had any observations they want to share with you. You can also volunteer something you might do differently next time.

- "I'm glad we got to agreement on the company sales strategy. In the spirit of learning, do you have any feedback on how I could improve my negotiating skills? I'm always looking to get better."
- Always start with something positive. Any good manager knows about the feedback sandwich—that is, offering up a strength, a weakness, and then another strength so that someone can really hear constructive input. You can apply the same idea in giving feedback. It also shows more credibility in that your counterpart believes you're analyzing things in a balanced but not one-sided way.
  - "I don't know where you learned to close a deal like that but you're really skilled at bringing lots of loose ends to a clear conclusion. Still, one thing I had a hard time with was . . . "
- Offer constructive criticism with as much goodwill as you would in delivering it to a daughter, son, niece, nephew, or other child you care about. You want the person to grow from this information, not be seared by it.
  - "I've always enjoyed our working relationship, but it bothered me today when you said my department's needs didn't matter."
- Keep your observations just that—things you actually saw—and actively look to keep them focused on behaviors, not on intent or motivation. Don't imprint your stylistic preferences on the other person; instead, use respectful negotiation as a marker everyone should be aiming for.
  - "I knew we were here to talk about the problems with the new timesheet system, so I was surprised and disappointed when you kept making remarks that were personally disparaging, like when you said . . . "
- As you deliver feedback, be sensitive to the other side's feelings, but not to the extent that it stops you from sharing or

paralyzes you altogether. Don't leave an important piece of feedback unsaid.

- "When you abruptly walked out of the room, I felt like I didn't matter and this issue wasn't worth settling in your eyes. Can you tell me where you were coming from?"

Of course, asking for a feedback exchange means you'll be hearing it as well as delivering it—and this is a great thing, if not always easy. Lori A. Greenawalt, partner at KPMG LLP, points out the role feedback has played in her career.

"In life, not just in my profession, going through good and bad situations has been imperative. When I get positive feedback, I ask myself, 'Why did I get it now? Did I do something different?' Sometimes I really have to evaluate the situation closely because it feels like I've been doing the same thing for years." Still, Lori advises a balanced approach. "The thing about being reflective is that there is a balance between hearing feedback to grow and become more effective, and listening so much to your own mental noise that it becomes defeating. Don't live inside your head. Don't take things too personally. You know who you are, you know where you've been, you've considered the feedback from others and hopefully you know where your opportunities lie. Reflection is good, but don't be so introspective that you become immobile."

Receiving feedback constructively means balancing an openness to the content with enough emotional distance that you really hear what's being said. Irene Chang Britt, chief strategy officer at Campbell Soup Company, advises, "When you get negative feedback, it's just one piece of interesting information. It's not everything. Remember, it's not how far you fall but how high you bounce." Fizzah Jafri, COO, Fixed Income Research and Economics at Morgan Stanley, offers, "The skill of hearing feedback isn't necessarily something we develop in college. I arrived in a fast-paced environment that had a low tolerance for errors, where no one had any time. That's made me quite direct. I expect someone to hear my take on something and if they don't like it, they need to either push back or move on. . . . If you fall apart at the sight of conflict, you won't advance very much in your career. While something may be hard to hear, usually it's not a personal insult."

CONFIRM THE TERMS

Following your own self-analysis—and a feedback exchange if it's appropriate—you must validate what you heard in the meeting. This kind of follow-up helps you clarify and fortify positions once they've been finalized. Even if you need to have another conversation or get information from a third party, it's still imperative that you sum up what was discussed—first at the close of the meeting and then afterward in writing. Closing the meeting by explicitly reviewing what was agreed upon and what the next steps will be gives both of you a chance to focus your thinking, minimize misunderstandings, and make any clarifications if needed. When you follow up with a version of that summary in writing, and if your counterpart denies any of the terms of the negotiation (or altogether leaves the company), you have some form of proof of your discussion.

Let's say you just discussed a reduced work arrangement with your boss. You might close the conversation in a way that sets the stage for your follow-up. "So to summarize, you're comfortable with me reducing my hours to twenty hours per week and moving to an hourly rate of my current salary. However you need to double-check with HR on whether or not my 401K will be affected. I'll need to check back in with you next Tuesday and you can expect an e-mail from me summarizing what we talked about."

Putting the terms of a discussion in writing, even if it's just e-mail, is the next step. Taking the responsibility to do this allows you to fashion the terms as you heard them, which is always more advantageous than letting someone else summarize them and risking having to conform to what your counterpart heard. Whether your negotiation was a phone call, an in-person meeting, or a large group roundtable discussion, safeguard yourself by proactively writing up what you heard and circulating it to those you negotiated with.

MULLING A DECISION OVER

One of the scenarios you'll likely find yourself in is the postnegotiation think-through. If you've been made an offer or presented with deal terms, you'll want to give yourself plenty of time to think through the proposal. Before, I told you there is power in silence, and the same thing applies when you take time to consider your options. You may feel tempted to give a quick answer or to be seen as less of an inconvenience but asking for time is expected and fair. Be ready when receiving job offers, for example, for the other side to pressure you with manufactured due dates and a quick need to know where you stand.

You want to be careful during this time to be neutral and respectful rather than conveying false agreement or contrition with terms. By doing so, you'll preserve your reputation and integrity. You can save a more personalized approach, when you may choose to reveal more, for when the deal is complete.

HANDLING "NO"

As you do your share of negotiating, you will face rejections, negative responses, and even situations when someone gives you a "yes," only to later overturn it. That's more than okay. Rebecca Baker, chief marketing officer and global partner, Alvarez & Marsal, says,

"Progress isn't made in an uninterrupted, upward trajectory. You will learn the most from when you're tested, when you've suffered at the hands of defeat or rejection. When I heard 'no' to potential new jobs or areas of responsibility, I came away with so much learning. Rejection is instructive; it helps you right-size what and who you really are." What's more, Liz Lange, founder and creative director of Liz Lange Maternity, notes, "Shut out naysayers completely. There will always be people saying that you're wrong." Indeed, hearing "no" means that your sights are set high, just where they should be. Linda Babcock and Sara Laschever, coauthors of *Ask for It*, have gone so far as to say, "If you never hear 'no,' then you're not asking for enough."[1]

On Making Lemons into Lemonade

"When I was getting my MBA, following the first semester of the first year, I was sent one of those letters that went out to fifteen people, suggesting I might not want to come back. My grades weren't where they needed to be. Distraught, I went to see my advisor. An accountant by background, my advisor was one tough cookie. When I showed him the letter, he said, 'Are you just going to slither away? The school said you might want to leave, not that you have to! Now get out there and change their minds.' That talk really helped me turn things around. I ended up graduating on the dean's honor list. Later my advisor told me, 'I knew it. I knew coddling wouldn't have worked with you. I just had to push your pride button.'"

—Irene Chang Britt, chief strategy officer at Campbell Soup Company

---

What we do know for sure is that "no" can mean many things. "'No' doesn't always mean 'no,'" says DeeDee Wilson, SVP of finance at L.L.Bean. "Often a woman who gets a 'no' will think, 'I shouldn't talk about it anymore. I should drop it.' Men, on the other hand, see a 'no' and think, 'They're not ready or they're not interested today, but it's not that they don't like the idea.' Being persistent is so important. If I get pushback, I let it sit for a while, then come back to it and try it again. I try to ask, 'Is this really a 'no' or just a lack of interest in having this conversation today?'"

A negative response can be tied to the fact that your counterpart stubbed her toe getting out of bed this morning, just discovered his partner is having an affair, or has a colicky newborn that's keeping her from getting a decent night's sleep. The possibilities, having something or nothing at all to do with your particular issue, are endless. Setbacks are to be expected but I hope you'll choose to see them as delays, rather than dead ends. Fizzah Jafri reassures, "For the record, any woman who's been successful has had setbacks. I'd bet most of them have had an outside person who oriented them again and brought back equilibrium."

Hear "No" as "Not Yet"

Much of what drives a "no" may be out of your control; what's not out of your control is the ability to take "no" as "not yet." Realize that a dead-end response is rarely an absolute or final answer in the negotiating realm. Choosing to interpret "no" as "not yet" helps you invent new and different options and can also have a big impact on your own morale and ability to keep reaching high.

When you get a "no," you can show your persistence by keeping the momentum of your ask going. April Carty-Sipp, SVP of creative services, Comcast Sports Group, says, "You can even use hearing 'no' to your advantage. You might say, 'I've gotten pushback on four consecutive ideas in a row. I'd really like you to look at this one.'" If you're told you're not ready for a promotion, for example, you can come up with a handful of concrete follow-up actions you can take. You might put a reminder in your calendar to approach your boss several months from now or decide you will do further research to make your case more compelling. You could also choose to throw out your first style of delivery altogether and consider a new, more tailored approach that could be even more effective. Sheila Murphy, associate general counsel at MetLife, notes, "Remember that budgets and circumstances change. Don't be afraid to bring your request up again."

Perhaps the best way of all to manage a setback is to use it as fuel and motivation. "I actually kept the binder of all the job rejections I received," says April Carty-Sipp. "In fact, I still have it. I thought those rejections could help me do better and they also kept me motivated. I knew I wouldn't always hear 'no.' At some point, someone would say 'yes.'" "Nos" are inevitable and universal; expect them and don't take them too personally.

STAY ORIENTED TOWARD THE POSITIVE

One of the most common—yet worst—effects of being told "no" is the tendency to become sour or toxic. Similarly, we might be tempted to triangulate, to give our friends and colleagues an earful about why our counterpart is lacking. "Sometimes women won't speak up in a meeting when they have an objection, but later they'll vent to others. I see this a lot. We need to be comfortable having a voice—publicly—otherwise our complaints are counterproductive.... You need to articulate your objection early on and then bounce back quickly. Don't dwell on issues. The 'complainer' perception tends to stick.... Become known as a constructive thinker," explains Fizzah Jafri.

When you show that you're a "glass-half-full" kind of employee, you instantly enhance your reputation as a problem solver. Susan

McFarland reasons, "Adaptability matters . . . because things always change. That's been a competitive advantage for me. Leaders will always appreciate an employee who gets to the new norm quicker. You should also help lead others there quickly, which can distinguish you." Susan expanded on this idea, stressing, "Attitude is so important. Show that you're a change enabler, not a roadblock. I'll take good attitude over skill any day."

You can also enhance your standing by being sure you discuss and spend time on what matters. "Don't hold a grudge . . . ever," cautions Lori A. Greenawalt. "It won't become you. Being part of the solution, rather than just discussing the problems, is a critical trait. The conversations that get spinning at big companies can waste a great deal of time and energy. If you're not part of the solution, then don't become part of the noise. Work to resolve it or don't get involved."

No matter who you are or what came out of your negotiation, you continually build on the reputation you already have. Make sure that you're doing that in a positive way, conveying that you're a relentless problem solver and committed to continual improvement.

STAY IN THE GAME

You won't always hear what you want, but if you have faith that you can change the minds of decision makers with time or added effort, then hang in there. "There's no room for acrimony in even the toughest conversations," says Lucy S. Danziger, editor-in-chief of *SELF Magazine.* "Be positive or neutral, otherwise you won't do your best work. There's always a way forward if you can resist isolating yourself. . . . Bring a team together to find a solution." If you've been dealt a disappointment in an ask that really mattered to you, try your best to stay engaged as an employee, focusing on where you're going and building your everyday credibility. Avoid at all costs what HR folks call the "stay but leave" phenomenon, where an employee shows up for work every day but barely participates. No one will be motivated to do what you want or give you something if your performance wanes.

Similarly, don't let the experience of being told "no" or hearing negative feedback send you into a poor self-esteem tailspin. "One setback made a big impression on me," recalls DeeDee Wilson. "In my first year as CFO of Nike Europe, I got feedback that I was a good director of finance but that I wasn't leading like a CFO needs to. The head CFO asked me, 'Have you ever failed before?' I was appalled—that remark must have confirmed that I was failing. I had to look deep and ask what they needed that they weren't getting. I eventually figured out what I needed to adjust: I had been so consumed with trying to be perfect technically that I was losing sight of being a leader. What I could change, I did. I shifted my organization and delegated some of the work and focused my energy where I was most helpful (and needed). I had a feeling in my gut that I could be successful at that job if I made some adjustments. Sometimes those setbacks are the very best thing for you. I was moving through the passages of leadership and I needed that kick in the right direction."

For each of us, there are other moments, such as when you're rejected, when you don't want to hang in there or when you can see nothing's going to change. You may decide, for example, after having been passed over for a role, that the prospect of additional jobs opening up in the near future looks unlikely. If your BATNA is a good one, there is nothing wrong with walking away from a broken situation that you don't foresee becoming functional.

> ## On Moving Up by Moving Out
>
> "While a managing director at an investment management firm in New York, I found myself at a point where I had topped out. While it wasn't a bad place to be, I wanted to have more impact. I knew that a colleague, John, was near retirement. I sat down with my boss and my boss's boss and asked if I could take over John's biggest client; I wanted his job. While I was excited and hopeful, in the end, I never heard back from them. I decided to channel that excitement into a new opportunity, and I landed the job I have now, working as the CEO of Calvert Investments. When I gave my resignation at my old firm, an executive said to me, 'Why didn't you tell me you wanted to run something?' I was incredulous. Realize that you can always fire your boss and quit. You have a lot more power than you realize."
>
> —Barbara J. Krumsiek, president, CEO, and chair of Calvert Investments, Inc.

Starting a job search would certainly be a way to empower yourself—to move up by moving out. To be sure, one way we negotiate is by leaving! Marie Chandoha, president and CEO, Charles Schwab Investment Management, discusses exactly this idea when she cautions, "As you enter the workforce, you will encounter situations where you will see gender inequity play out. Early on, when I saw something unfair, I didn't have as thick of a skin for handling it. The point is, there are different firms out there and some are more open to women than others. I would like to have known that sooner."

One interesting yet mistaken belief endures about executive level women. Many of us think they consistently got things right and never struggled professionally. In fact every woman I interviewed shared stories of setbacks, rejections, and slammed doors on their way to the top. Just consider the experience of Rebecca Baker. "As a marketer," she notes, "my leaders depend on me to come up with new and innovative ideas. Mind you, some of these ideas will never see the light of day and some will succeed. Just because an idea may not be chosen doesn't mean you should be deterred from trying again." Similarly, Rosemary Turner recalls, "One of my bosses, a president at the time, told me that the furthest I would ever climb was the VP level. She explained, giving reasons I disagreed with, that I wasn't 'president' material. That experience ended up being really motivating. I started to network internally quite a bit, realizing I was going to need to advocate for myself. Not only did I pursue the top job anyway, but I got promoted to president four months later. I'm someone who considers *myself* the master of my own career."

On Handling Setbacks

"It's hilarious to me to think of a successful person not having setbacks. That said, I personally don't understand the glass ceiling or the idea that we as women can't reach for what we want.

As an entrepreneur, I hear 'no' all the time. I'm always proposing new things and the fact is, no one really likes change. Mind you, not all 'nos' are external. We often tell ourselves 'no.' I see that women can be hardest on themselves. Believe in yourself. If you get rejected, just try a new avenue.

No woman—or man—will go far if easily discouraged."

—Liz Lange, founder and creative director of Liz Lange Maternity

---

Lucy Danziger takes a more investigative approach. "The most important thing when you get turned down is to figure out why. Focus on getting to 'yes' the next time by uncovering the reason for 'no.' Look deeply at your counterpart's point of view and don't get angry; instead, try to understand. If you want to be a leader, there's no room for recrimination. At every stage in your career, be respectful, civil, decent, and professional. You can also handle 'no' by infusing some humor and lightheartedness into the situation."

However you choose to handle setbacks, realize that leaders who tell you "no" will look for persistence in you. After all, we often expect people to push back when we make our initial offer or tell them we couldn't possibly go "that low." When I negotiate with new client companies to come in and do a speech, for example, contacts will inevitably ask me what I charge. Mind you—my quote is designed to be negotiated—so I'm routinely surprised that only about 5 percent of clients negotiate my fees with me. Know that when someone says "no" or offers you something they are most likely expecting some resistance or a different viewpoint on your part. Show them that you're not afraid of a little back-and-forth.

DON'T DROP THE CONNECTION

A big part of being resilient is showing your counterpart that you still have a right to interface with him or her and make future requests even if you hear "no" or don't get the initial answer you want. As an entrepreneur, I've seen many times when a person is *too willing* to back down quickly. For example, people are selling to me all the time, whether they're speaking agents, graphic designers, marketing professionals, or other small business specialists. Interestingly, I notice that I am pursued quite forcefully as I'm being sold to, but the minute I decline in favor of another vendor or out of disinterest, I'm treated with as much appeal as last week's leftover meatloaf. This is shortsighted and unnecessary. Even if I'm not a customer now, I could be one later.

Show your persistence by remaining engaged with your counterpart. Continue to keep the relationship and the topic warm by doing something counterintuitive: instead of asking for something more, focus on giving. Send your counterpart resources that can help them be better professionally or be more in the know. Forward them a relevant event advertisement, a helpful article, or interesting resource. Doing so shows that you're not afraid of a little thing called *rejection*. In fact, you're determined to build a relationship and you have shown yourself as generous and knowledgeable. When someone says "no" to what you're selling, show appreciation, and assure them that there will, in fact, be a next time and that they haven't seen the last of you.

Marie Chandoha reflects, "I'm a pretty persistent person. I've observed something interesting in watching professional sports. When a referee makes a call that's seen as unfair, players may not like it but tend to bounce back very quickly. They are pretty resilient when faced with a disappointment. In games—and at work—there's always something happening that you don't like. A woman might take that disappointment a lot more personally or seriously, thinking, 'That's the end, I'm finished.' It's not a bad thing to say instead, 'Let's move on.'"

As well, we can show faith in ourselves by knowing we're worthy to make contact with top leaders and high-ranking, could-be mentors, no matter how much more senior they are than us. "I do a lot of work with horses and what I've learned is that in a herd, there's always one dominant animal," continues Marie. "I've noticed that a new horse will have a short interaction with the leader rather early on and periodically later on. Those interactions determine how the horses stack up in the pecking order. It's not a drawn-out or continual interaction, though; there isn't a need to keep asserting power. We can learn something valuable from this approach. Each of us wants to know, 'How do you enter a new herd and become the lead horse?'"

DON'T BE AFRAID TO TOUGHEN UP

One thing we know for sure is that negotiations would be simpler without emotions creeping into the mix. But, alas, that's as likely as losing weight by eating cheesecake and donuts. So, to navigate the world of asking for what you want, it'll help you to start toughening up. I don't mean that you need to become callous, unfeeling, or dead inside. I mean that you need to learn to make requests and deal with the aftermath in a way that's not deeply personalized and internalized.

"You must have a thick skin," says Fizzah Jafri. "Mine is a very intense and demanding industry. You must be able to deal with criticism in this environment. There is low tolerance for mistakes. No one will say, 'I don't think you did this right.' They will be a little more direct! In these situations, you either have to own up to a mistake or defend your position. If you did make a mistake, it's important to say, 'I was off in my thinking.' People respect that and are more likely to give you a chance in the future if you can acknowledge when you're wrong." Fizzah went on to warn, "You can't take things personally in a business environment. I know that if I left my company, I would be replaced in two weeks and the firm would keep going."

One way we can think of a thick skin is in terms of adaptability. Truly adaptable leaders have springy reflexes, meaning that they can fall and then bounce, pivot, or creatively maneuver their way through problems. Adaptability also means putting your attention where it's needed—on what you can influence—rather than wasting time stuck in the past. Liz Lange shares, "Early on, if someone didn't like my products or something that I did, I ruminated on it. I'd stay up all night writing an e-mail response, explaining why I was sorry or why something had happened. My husband at the time said to me, 'It's no big deal. You can't make that person happy.' I can see that he was right. If I get a crazy ranting e-mail today from someone who's really dissatisfied, I'm more collected about it. Sometimes I'll say to that person, 'Every brand isn't for everybody and everybody isn't for every brand.'"

When we project toughness, we can more easily succeed as the sole woman in the room, the one going against the popular approach, or the one who can do something difficult. For example, Carol Ann

Petren, executive vice president and general counsel, MacAndrews & Forbes Holdings Inc., recommends, "Focus on the issue and not the person—it is rarely a good thing to damage a relationship in the process of negotiating." April Carty-Sipp elaborates on this, noting, "You don't want to be seen as too sensitive. Realize that so much in business can be misinterpreted or overthought. Everything is not personal." Balancing our desire for likeability with our desire to get our agenda met is, therefore, a career advancement requirement.

KEEP EXPANDING THE PIE

A fantastic thing happens when you make an ask and achieve your preferred outcome or make good progress. You will want to up the ante. As Catherine Ann Mohan, partner and treasurer at McCarter & English, explains, "I always try to negotiate ways I can make a greater impact with my clients. If I'm doing work for a national company, for example, I may ask them to tell me about their legal problems outside of the case we're dealing with at hand. I'm comfortable saying 'I can do more for you.' As women, it's really important that we do more of this, actively expanding our business, client base, or work responsibilities. You need to do it for yourself and for your business."

In addition to asking for more, we can also approach renewed or ongoing negotiations with increased fervor. Many of the executives I interviewed expressed that they can be bolder or more aggressive with those they negotiate with often. Why? Ongoing negotiations give us the advantage of knowing what to expect. For example, our counterpart's style and dominant preferences become much easier to predict. If the opposite occurs, however, and it feels like we've hit a dead end, one way that we can reinvigorate ongoing negotiations is by adding a new party. By adding diverse constituents to a tired conversation, including people in other functions, outsiders, or subject matter experts, you can unleash exactly the creativity that's been lacking in a negotiation.

Once a negotiation has happened, you can also proactively conduct an eight-week inspection to see how whatever's been agreed on is working. By taking the initiative to evaluate a negotiated agreement, you can more quickly shift gears or make improvements. Similarly, you can hold yourself and others accountable, continuing to invent options and ideas to enhance the offering that's already on the table.

Although you may leave a negotiation feeling as though you prospered—for example, if you received a promotion over a colleague—it doesn't mean you shouldn't continue to build the relationship with your counterpart. "If I get pushback, I don't take it personally or see it as a battle with one winner and one loser," says Linda Descano, president and CEO of Women & Co., a program of Citibank. "I try to respectfully present my argument, and be gracious if it goes my way, and remain upbeat if it doesn't. If I do win, I will keep building bridges with the people who feel like they lost."

IT'S A SMALL WORLD AFTER ALL

Realize that your reputation as a worker and a negotiator will follow you. That means seeing your relationships in a longitudinal way and having the foresight to understand that the power balance that exists between two parties today might look very different in the future. "I've negotiated with some of the most successful lawyers in the country," remembers Catherine Ann Mohan. "It's important to be tough but respectful and remember that the world is round. If you mistreat someone now, a year later you might find yourself having to deal with them again."

What kind of reputation have you created as a negotiator? Even if we're playing a secondary, supporting role in a negotiation, we still leave a footprint. In fact, often the way we conduct ourselves when things are getting contentious between two parties is illustrative of how we'll be judged by others. Sheila Murphy says, "Once there was a battle of power going on between two individuals I worked with, a peer and a client. In the midst of a re-org, one of them was perceived as losing, and one of them was seen as the winner. I was clear that I would be neutral, particularly because in a time of turmoil, people assume you'll pick a side. I treated both people with the same respect and dignity. A year later the person who 'lost' found himself in a much higher position than his counterpart! You just never know where people you work with and negotiate with will end up. In a situation where you're in the middle, both sides are watching you carefully. Don't burn any bridges." When you negotiate—and follow up—with respect, honesty, and assertiveness, you don't have to worry about where your counterparts will end up one year from now or whether you need to negotiate with them again.

Never Stop Building the Trust

As you navigate the aftereffects of asking for what you want, don't be afraid to show your persistence; always remaining constructive. What's more, your ability to be positive and imaginative will often generate supporters for your cause without you even knowing it. At each turn, remember to thank the people who supported you, advised you, or negotiated with you.

What's more, keep the big picture in mind. What you accomplished in one negotiation isn't reflective one iota of what's possible in the future. As April Carty-Sipp explains, "You're not always going to be right or win every argument. As long as you make progress, that's what's important. If you don't get what you want, it'll help you next time to sell your idea in a new way. What I've learned over the years is that it's hard for people to say 'no' to you constantly."

At its essence, asking for something we want is about having a voice. When we advocate on our own behalf, we know that we're deserving of good things, that we're smart enough to handle whatever unfolds at the negotiating table, and that we only get what we ask for. We can all learn from Linda Descano, who has found a very healthy sense of worthiness in herself: "I really respect myself. There's a lot I'm not, but I appreciate my strengths. I know deep down that I have something to offer, something of value. No one is going to take that away from me."

7

Push Back to Own Your Career

When I look around, I can count on one hand the people I know who would say they're really living their dreams. I have to wonder, why isn't it more the norm to have what you want? Why is it so very commonplace to conform to our work environments, squelching the full level of talent we can contribute? Why should you *not* live your dream? As we broaden and expand our negotiating and advocating skills, we can steer our careers in exactly the direction we want.

If in your own life you're toying with making a change, taking a chance, or going for an opportunity, do it. The learning, regardless of the outcome, will make it worth it. If you're willing to risk and negotiate, you'll take control of your future and create a life for yourself free of unspoken wishes, regrets, or unmanaged burdens. This life skill will fill your life with as many of your aspirations as you conceive.

You'll probably remember the interview question I cited in Chapter One when I asked participants to quantify the impact of pushing back. I asked interviewees, "Assuming a woman's career success equals 100 percent, what percentage is accounted for by her effectiveness in negotiating and pushing back?"

Averaging the twenty responses I heard, the answer was 60 percent; that's to say that 60 percent of a woman's career success hinges on her pushback skills—holding her own, advocating her needs, and negotiating. Negotiating skills are absolutely basic to pushback, and we've spent the last few chapters really breaking down the four steps of a well-conducted negotiation, from preparation to follow-up. These skills, along with the other pushback-related skills and traits—self-advocacy, action taking, resiliency, seeking the right help, and more—are also crucial to advancing our careers. These skills and traits, when we practice and nurture them in ourselves, feed on one another so that our abilities and our confidence take off.

That's what we'll talk about in this chapter: using and building our pushback skills to claim total ownership of our careers. Maneuvering through office politics with savvy, acting in spite of a recent failure, and being strategic about inserting ourselves into opportune situations that can propel us. We'll see how our responses to our most glittering successes and our most public mistakes can be as important as the daily reputation we carve out on the job and the way in which we treat colleagues. You'll also see a common vein that distinguishes those professionals seen as "leadership material." It's not that they're consistently the smartest in the room, perpetually unafraid, or blessed with good fortune; rather, they position themselves well by getting help when they need it and being savvy about their environments. Let's see just what it is they know that others don't.

On Taking Action

"For fourteen years, I worked somewhere where I was never asked to go out and get business. I had one big client that represented 90 percent of my work. Then one day, that client went bankrupt. I was a partner at the time—forty-two years old—with twin daughters and a stay-at-home husband. As the breadwinner, I was panicked when a senior partner said to me, "You have to bring in some business within the next six months or find another job.."

It took me two full weeks to get out from under my feeling of desperation.

Then after a tough but motivating chat with my father, I got out my rolodex. Starting with the A's, I called everyone I knew, telling them I would try any kind of case, help them with anything, or travel anywhere. When I got to the letter G, I came across a small company that was getting sued. They asked if I'd try their case in Baltimore. Even though the job was small, I was overjoyed. I wasn't going to turn down anything.

Over time, I developed a lot of business for that company and I was able to use that experience to open a regional office for my current firm.

Even though lots of people said 'no' to me, I kept in touch with them. I never give up."

—Catherine Ann Mohan, partner and treasurer at McCarter & English

Overcoming Inertia

There's a kernel to asking that involves moving from inaction—the place where we often complain and fret—to action, the spot where we're actually doing something about our issue. This movement is important in your career because there will be numerous situations that could serve to paralyze you, stilling your ambition, and quieting your hopes. You will be rejected by someone, hear "no," be told you're not ready, not qualified, or have a door slammed in your face. That's a guarantee, so expect it.

And yet, for lots of us, the hardest part of this rejection isn't experiencing it in the first place, it's moving forward from it. We need to take a risk, move ahead, and recover anyway—in spite of the nonvalidation we've gotten—proceeding only with faith in ourselves. A case in point: so many of the people I meet when giving talks explain to me that they feel stuck in their careers. When I ask what they're doing to test other opportunities or move out of atrophy, they tell me they're "thinking" about it. Thinking is all well and good (I think you know by now that I'm a proponent of self-analysis), but it won't move your actual goals forward one bit without action. Expect moments that will test you and you won't be so handicapped by them. See risky opportunities as made of rubber, not of glass. Have high expectations of yourself as resilient and get accountability partners, those close enough to call you on nonaction or disengagement from your goals and who help you continue onward. Don't be one of those people who spends her lifetime planning for a risk, dreaming about change, or plotting to do something huge. Promise yourself that when adversity comes knocking, you'll swivel, shift, pivot, try something new—as long as you keep moving!

SEE YOURSELF AS A CHANGE AGENT

Yet another approach to keep in mind as you encounter pushback scenarios of different sizes and levels of significance is to notice the ongoing element of change. Asking for something new or advocating for an alternate way will require a modification in how it's done.

That's the case whether you're asking for more money or to have your company's maternity leave policy revised to be more flexible. The process of change management, although typically thought of on a grand scale—like shifting to a new business model across a large organization—can actually be called on in everyday situations.

Cindi Bigelow, president of Bigelow Tea, recalls her own history of asking for change, noting, "I had to pitch pretty hard to get the positions I've held in this company. What helped me to rise in the ranks was to not make promotions about me and my advancement, but to make it about the company. I sold it as, 'Move me into this role and I can get new things done for the business and get us to an even better place.'"

Truly savvy change agents are adept at creating momentum where there's none. To do that, pioneering types use a process that can convincingly demonstrate future potential and sustainability. They often create a coalition of like-minded people—being transparent about their motivations—and use the influence they have to harness a change. They also paint a vivid picture of potential or what *could be*. A stepped system, like the following, can help guide your next change initiative:

1. *Show the costs of inaction:* Only when we define *how it is*, also known as the baseline, can we provide contrast about *how it could be.* Demonstrate how the current state of the situation you want to change is affecting you, the company, the staff, the customers, and any other noteworthy stakeholders.

2. *Solicit input:* You can stimulate people's thinking by involving them in roundtable discussions, town hall–style meetings, or even focus groups. Perhaps even more important, you'll show that you care how change will affect others. A side benefit to soliciting input is that you'll get greater buy-in—and maybe even pick up some unexpected champions—of your cause.

3. *Garner support:* You can generate excitement by building momentum and enthusiasm around the change. By communicating progress with people and reinvolving them when needed, you can brand the change proactively and keep others' voices in the discussion. You'll want to demonstrate any short-term quick wins early on through examples and success stories.

4. *Make the change stick:* If you want to keep your initiative thriving, then you'll need to keep it close to your most important stakeholders. Even if your change is implemented, you can reward behavior that aligns with the change through public praise or other forms of recognition. Making the initiative real to people by showing a larger, global impact can help immensely.

5. *Operationalize the change:* Once a change has been institutionalized, it's easier to hold people accountable to it. Accountability may mean reeducating people or ensuring that recognition is given for compliance and conversely that penalties exist for those who won't cooperate. You can and should continually solicit feedback on the change to keep it dynamic and evolving in people's eyes.

Demonstrating early gains can make all the difference to resisters. "Allow people to be part of the process," Cindi Bigelow notes. "If they do not agree, they have to be able to share that with you. You need to listen and include those thoughts in the development of a process or plan or product. It has sometimes taken years to move my team forward on concepts that were very new and made the group uncomfortable. That might seem time consuming but when I have invested the time to get everyone on board, they got behind the concept with so much more energy and focus." Managing—and asking for—change are easier when we understand the forces that build buy in and those that decimate it.

Change Management Aids

- *Be ready for pushback:* Show self-awareness and self-management, knowing your buttons may get pushed.
- *Have environmental awareness:* Key into the organization's culture and past success stories of change.
- *Set your own bar high:* Don't rationalize poor practices and behaviors.
- *Be a glass-half-full kind of person:* Model that you see change as an opportunity, not as an obstacle.

Don't be shy; go ahead and lead a change. The success of a change initiative can positively brand you in ways that nothing else can. In one of the most compelling examples I've witnessed, Catherine, an HR associate at a medium-sized firm, zeroed in on a change she wanted to advocate. Catherine was passionate about environmental issues and noticed, to her disappointment, areas in which the company was being wasteful. She decided to propose a green taskforce that would work internally to eliminate inefficient processes and reduce the firm's overall footprint.

As Catherine went unassumingly about her change strategy, using a process similar to the one described in this chapter, she found in the end she had changed her reputation permanently. After assembling her taskforce, Catherine began reporting to the chief operating officer on green opportunities for improvement as well as the areas in which the firm was excelling. She called on new skills, leading and creating a vision for the taskforce, conducting considerable research, and carefully pitching ideas to management, even when she wondered if she was the best qualified as the head of the group. Perhaps, best of all, as changes were being implemented, Catherine was the one who sent monthly e-mail updates to all company staff, including usage and savings to the company. Her visibility skyrocketed, she was now associated with being a pioneer and saving the company money, and she was pretty unanimously deemed "leadership material." No one was surprised a few months later when Catherine was promoted to a management position.

As we can learn from Catherine, the best changes are ones for which we have a particular passion. What's more, a well-matched opportunity is one in which we can maximize a group's strengths to move the organization ahead. Says Cindi Bigelow, "I continue to keep the focus on what I can do for the organization that isn't being addressed and believe I've been successful because I put the business first, above personalities, egos, or anything else."

If a change project doesn't work out, in fact, *when* it doesn't work out, you have a great opportunity to call on your own resilience mind-set. Certainly, if you're butting up against resistance or see a flaw in your approach, you'll be well served to pivot, repackage, or recommunicate your message. You might even go back to the drawing board altogether and do some research to understand what has made other change initiatives successful at your firm or within your industry. You'll notice that change agents don't sit on the sidelines waiting for others to do it; they choose their opportunities well, key into their own passion, and make it happen.

Regardless of the brand that you try to sculpt for yourself, I encourage you to make *continual improvement* two of the keywords that people associate with you. Once you engage in a change management process, making improvement synonymous with your name, you will notice that your political and social capital, among other benefits, dramatically increase.

GO AHEAD, BE AN OPPORTUNIST

A big piece of advancing in your career and a central part of self-advocacy is inserting yourself proactively in beneficial situations. Just as we tend to receive when we ask, we can find a gold mine of opportunity when we get up and actually place ourselves in a dealing that excites or interests us.

"The very first thing I did in college was take a job at the career development center, a role where I knew I'd be the first to see advertised jobs," recalls April Carty-Sipp, SVP of creative services, Comcast Sports Group. "One day, I saw an internship opportunity that entailed working for a professional sports team. I applied, even though I was the only female to do so, and got the job. What I knew back then is that you are your own best advocate. Be an opportunist! If you're not going to insert yourself in beneficial situations, apply for a great opportunity, or otherwise take a risk, you'll lose out. Other people shouldn't tell you how to manage your career; guide it yourself."

If this concept of being strategic makes you uncomfortable, think about the many microstrategies you can use to ease in. Can you ask to be included in an interesting assignment? Offer to take on a role that's outside of your domain? Be ready to chat up the CEO when you inevitably bump into him in the elevator? Those who ready and insert themselves into great situations tend to get noticed and be heard, all the while conveying their sense of ambition and drive.

Some of the following examples offer ripe opportunities to expand your impact at work:

- While serving on an internal committee, you offer to be the one who sends e-mails to the entire company updating them on progress made.

- You write to the editor of the company newsletter and ask her to include a recent success story or accolade you or your team received.

- You hear about a brand new opportunity while chatting with a peer in the hallway. You're immediately interested and you tell your peer then and there about your fervor to be part of it.

- You attend a networking event knowing a contact will be there whom you very much want to meet. In advance, you do research on this person and pointedly approach her at the function, coming prepared with good questions and a solid introduction.

The list of ways with which we can be strategic about broadening our visibility are limitless. Having a strategy is a smart practice and takes the onus off of others to read your mind. Susan McFarland, executive vice president and principal accounting officer at Capital One, explains, "We women like to be good at something, without having to draw attention to it. It seems to mean more to us when we get unsolicited kudos. But the truth is that you're putting too much burden on others when you don't ask for what you want. It's unfair to not be clear. Tell people where you stand, even if your stance is, 'I'm indifferent.'"

Often the reason people advance is that they demonstrate the competence level of the job they want, not the job they have. "You must be able to take a position, defend it, and advocate it. If you can't do that, you're not a leader," says Sheila Murphy, associate general counsel at MetLife. "Too many people just do their work. But you have to 'act the role' before you're given it. Even if you're not yet a leader, show that you can hold your ground and defend your point." In fact, your position or level in the organization doesn't have any bearing on how much of a leader you can be. Cindi Bigelow offers, "Understand that you need to be a role model regardless of the position you hold or the level where you sit. People are always watching so make sure you distinguish yourself as someone whom people can point to and say, '*That* I like. *That* I want to listen to.'"

The point here is that you will need to bank on advocating for your own involvement, not waiting for others to extend an invitation or to qualify you as the best person for the job. Fizzah Jafri, COO, Fixed Income Research and Economics at Morgan Stanley, explains, "You're only going to advance if you're really competent, if people know that fact and if they like you. If two people are doing the same good work and one is better at showcasing her accomplishments, the self-promoter will win out every time. If you write a great report, for example, you better make sure everyone is aware you wrote it.... You must not be shy about demonstrating your abilities and blowing your trumpet; as women we hesitate more than men to do this. I manage two hundred reports a day. If someone wants to get noticed, he or she needs to get on my radar. The burden is on the employee to share achievements." Expect that the buck starts and stops with you and you'll naturally assume the role of chief executive, chief marketer, and chief accountability officer of your own career.

BE IN THE SERVICE BUSINESS

An effective way to distinguish yourself on the job is to be seen as a positive, constructive champion of the company. This is especially important today, when there are more candidates than jobs, and when companies can be choosy about who they keep and promote. When you take a service approach with your own coworkers, bosses, peers, and clients, you anticipate their needs and find quick answers to problems. At the same time, you end up branding yourself as someone who's not interested in complaining but rather in doing, someone who can be counted on to get things done and find answers.

April Carty-Sipp talks about this career tactic, explaining, "I have a positive outlook. I'm generally upbeat and happy, even if I don't get what I need. That can translate well to problem solving. I make a point to never approach my superiors with problems unless I have solutions. I've found this boosts my credibility because it takes some of the edge and pressure off of my managers."

Liz Lange, founder and creative director of Liz Lange Maternity, shared her perspective on being positive from the view of a boss, citing, "I choose to focus on solutions—not problems. When I used to manage over fifty employees I would arrive at work in the morning, for example, and there were lots of people lined up outside of my office. They were not there to tell me that fabric would be delivered early or that pricing had come in under budget. They were there to give me bad news. I always say, 'Don't come to me with a problem, come to me with a solution.'"

Those gifted at being service professionals know that giving others a voice is a quick way to earn appreciation and respect. Still, often we don't ask because we don't want to know the answers. Karen Ganzlin, chief human resources officer at TD Ameritrade, suggests being proactive anyway. "You have to be resilient if you want a big career. In getting feedback, you need to have a level of emotional intelligence to ask, accept, and then take action on the feedback in an effort to get better. . . . Recognize that difficult business decisions have to sometimes be made and that you can't take everything personally." Certainly, this kind of solicitation of feedback isn't always easy. Linda Descano, president and CEO of Women & Co., a program of Citibank, notes, "I get 360-degree feedback from my coworkers and that can be tough. The first time I was evaluated and given my results, I spent the night crying in my hotel room. I felt really embarrassed. The second time I said, 'This is really interesting.' You have to keep asking for feedback." Asking for input, even when you're afraid of what you'll hear, will always make you more effective and powerful, not less so, and it's when we'll need to call on our positive mind-set most!

Part of the legacy you can leave is that you treated people well regardless of their level. Rosemary Turner, president of Chesapeake UPS, does this, noting, "I've tried leading with just authority, but that got boring pretty quickly. When that didn't feel good, I made it a point to focus on building influence. Since then, I've prided myself on having relationships with people at all levels. I speak to drivers, for example, about what they need, rather than just shooing them to get on the road."

A positive, inclusive approach can keep you on track to go after what you really want. "I credit my cockeyed optimism as having helped me go far," says Liz Lange. "I'm not naive, but when you realize that most businesses fail, you have to really believe that despite odds, your business will flourish." Being persistently positive shows that you see change, for example, as an opportunity. It doesn't just benefit you, it models that constructive outlook for others, creating an infectious, widespread reaction. Become known as the inexorable problem solver—the truly positive, can-do up-and-comer—and it will be hard for leaders not to notice you.

Leave Some Room to F%$* It All Up

If you're going to make plans for a big career, then you had better create some space for the not-so-great to happen. When I asked Irene Chang Britt what she wished she'd known sooner in her career, she explained, "Not that I would have listened, but I wish I'd known that it was okay to make mistakes earlier in my career. I went on to make some real doozies but I wish that rather than being embarrassed, which I was, I appreciated it was all part of learning and developing on the job."

Indeed, mistakes are a major part of the passage of becoming a leader! We can't insist on guarantees, and much of the time we just have to improvise and live with the results. This kind of leap, the kind we take knowing that we'll grow our wings on the way down, is actually a skill. Karen Ganzlin recalls, "Looking at my career—I've been with the TD family of companies for twenty-nine years—I've moved twelve times, taking many different roles. When I was packing up in Toronto on a Friday night to come to work for TD Ameritrade in the United States that Monday, I just asked myself, 'What's the worst that can happen? I can always go back if it doesn't work out.' That kind of approach toward risk has always worked for me." Quelling and mitigating our own fears, just as Karen does, can make them look totally manageable as opposed to insurmountable. April Carty-Sipp cited a similar experience, explaining how she made the jump from one job to another. Assurance of perfect conditions is something no one can promise you when you take a risk. Acting anyway means getting past the need for that security. "I weigh the pros and cons of something and then decide if I should take a risk. For me, switching jobs was a big risk. I worked at another company for almost seven years. I loved my job but it became clear that my boss wasn't going anywhere. In fact, she's still in her same role today. With no growth prospects, I applied to and accepted another job at Comcast. After being here for ten years, I know that I made the right choice. You might not get what you need where you are. Don't be afraid to go find the challenge you want elsewhere."

Taking a chance and then allowing the possibility of failure is a gift you can extend to others, too, particularly those you manage. "Sometimes when I'm getting lots of pushback on an issue, like from someone I manage, for example, I'll allow them to do it their way even if I have my doubts," counsels Rosemary Turner. "Later I'll ask them, 'How did that go for you? Did it go the way you wanted?' I lead in a way that allows for some failure. As long as you don't make the same mistake twice, it's okay for my people to not always get things perfect." Perfection is more an enemy than a friend; in fact, banking on flawlessness will leave you squandering your ideas and talent.

MENTORS, SPONSORS, AND SAGES

I've shared in this book the value of engaging sponsors and mentors as you prepare for and follow up negotiations. But enlisting this group in your total career progression is equally necessary. Many of us will cite the scarcity of our time, our discomfort asking for help, or our worry that we're bothering "someone important" as key reasons why we don't do this. In fact, Lori A. Greenawalt, partner at KPMG LLP, was quite candid when she shared, "As I navigated my career, I didn't reach out to others like I should have because I didn't think I needed them or thought it would make me look weak or lacking in some way."

Lori has since changed her approach, tapping into the talent that's around her. "Now, if someone is more successful than me at something, I eagerly ask for their help working through specific items. If someone is more successful at handling difficult conversations with clients, for example, I'll say, 'This was how my last tough conversation unfolded.'"

Remember that the teaching mentors provide is just one element of what they can give you. Be certain that at least some of your mentors are sponsors, that is, they are empowered to act on your behalf and help you and are committed to your success. "What I didn't realize early on is that every workplace is political," says Fizzah Jafri. "Just because people like you or enjoy you doesn't mean they'll vouch for you. That surprised me. If I regularly exchange pleasantries with someone, there's no guarantee that he or she will pound the table for my promotion."

To be sure, mentors and sponsors can give you the feedback that no one else is willing to share with you. They, in the spirit of seeing you grow and develop, can often position and deliver this information in a way that you can really hear it. Engaging one of these guides doesn't need to resemble a long, thought-out marriage proposal. Simply look for someone with whom you have an organic connection, whom you naturally admire, and ask for his or her time.

A forgotten but important piece of mentorship is making sure that you become one, too. Act as a pushback mentor for someone else, recognizing, for example, the young newcomer who never volunteers her ideas or always nods her head in agreement. "You can count on one thing: you don't get what you don't ask for," encourages Susan McFarland. "I've seen that play out time and again. Women need a little more pushing. Speak up. *Ask.* If you're good at asking, pull it out of other women who aren't by asking them, 'What do you want? Where are you looking to go?'" One of the greatest sources of power is helping others to feel powerful, too.

REFUSING, REBUFFING, AND SAYING "NO"

We can't just be prepared to hear the occasional "no" in our careers; we also want to be comfortable saying "no" when a situation doesn't meet our needs. There's clearly an art to doing this well because we don't want to turn people off from approaching us in the future or be seen as out only for ourselves. Still, you can say "no" more than you think—to job opportunities, certain assignments, volunteer experiences, and many other requests that don't fit your vision, goals, or workload. "You can say 'no,' but you should explain why," Marie Chandoha, president and CEO, Charles Schwab Investment Management, recommends. "You should show your commitment and desire to move forward. I remember working in a U.S. based role when my employer wanted me to move into a global role.

Given my family commitments at the time—when I couldn't travel extensively—I had to say, 'I can't do this now, but I'd love to do it in a few years.' Showing your commitment and interest is so important. Years later, I took the global role." Similarly, Linda Descano encourages women not to stop articulating their goals. "Don't assume people know your intent. If you liked an assignment but couldn't fit it in once, be sure that in every follow-up conversation, you reiterate that although timing wasn't right at first, you remain interested."

Indeed, it can leach our authority when we answer something with anything but "no" if it doesn't work for us. Deborah Simpson, chief financial officer of The Boston Consulting Group, shares that "the best advice I ever heard was that when you're too busy, always take on work that interests you. Somewhere, somehow, you'll sort out how to get the rest done. There are many career rewards for taking on meaty, tough assignments with complex problem-solving components; plus it'll be more enjoyable for you.... Don't sell yourself short; you're no different than anyone else who wants engaging work, so have a nose for searching it out!" Pinpointing and asking for what you love means saying "no" to what you don't want. Adds Darlene Slaughter, VP and chief diversity officer at Fannie Mae, "How you say 'no' and what you say 'no' to is everything. I've learned that when you say 'yes' to something and you mean 'no,' you lose your power. What will weaken you as a leader is to take on too many tasks that should be delegated. When ... you're saddled with busywork, people will leave you behind and keep moving forward."

Well, just which activities should we decline? "Sometimes, you have to give serious thought to whether the assignment will enhance your skills or best utilize your real value to the organization. If not, you have to be willing to take a pass—and it is always good to offer an alternative solution to getting the job done," advises Carol Ann

Petren, executive vice president and general counsel, MacAndrews & Forbes Holdings Inc. "Show that your 'no' is well thought out, with good reasons." Outside of your interests and goals, your own bandwidth can be the reason to decline an opportunity. Carol adds, "Being an overachiever, especially one who likes to be a team player, can be both a blessing and a curse. There is a natural inclination to say 'yes' to most requests, which is not always a good thing."

Saying "no" is also about challenging your manager or higher-ups when you strongly disagree. Mind you, this will go against every good-girlism you've ever known, but you can and need to do it. "We can and should say 'no,'" says April Carty-Sipp. "Good bosses will encourage you to disagree with them. Don't just be a 'yes' person." Throughout our careers, we will need to advocate for what we want, and then just as persuasively convince others why a different arrangement *isn't* right for us. You have more than enough permission to say 'no,' so start doing it.

MOVE ICE CUBES, NOT ICEBERGS

Many a career success story has been told about the bold risk taker, who, despite the odds and criticism of her idea, unearthed an amazing discovery or product. These major career milestones are exciting to listen to for the rest of us, an example of what's possible when you take a chance. But interestingly, the theme I heard in my interviews was that career success came from additive gains more than from winning a quick fifty-yard dash. Many women executives I met credited a slow-but-steady approach as having helped them build their reputations. Rather than trying to move an entire iceberg, these women "picked up ice cubes" one by one, making cumulative improvements and results. You, too, will see that there are many approaches, incremental in nature, which can get you where you want to be.

"What you'll find at the top is almost everyone's a high achiever," Karen Ganzlin reflects. "And yet, there's only so much you can do in so many hours. Things come up you don't anticipate and there are always emergencies. I think, too, many people focus on one grand slam in their careers when they should be concentrating on building momentum, which then leads to major breakthroughs." Perhaps we can get more from our everyday tasks than we realize. Rebecca Baker, chief marketing officer and global partner, Alvarez & Marsal, adds, "If you want a role that you have to grow into, understand that the daily blocking and tackling of a job can help you move forward more than you think. Depending on your workplace culture, gauge whether there are prescribed paths or if it's more entrepreneurial in nature. If there's no set trajectory, then by all means have open, honest conversations with your manager to get a better sense of how much initiative you can take." You can decide how you want to define career success, be it in gradual, baby steps or in colossal moves. But I think you'll find that the satisfaction of giving yourself daily challenges can give you far more sustained energy and endurance than the once-a-year victory.

A Model of Continual Improvement

Whether you're riding your highest high or recovering from your lowest low, self-analysis in your career is valuable. After all, very little in the work world—or in life for that matter—is black and white. "There's so much 'gray zone' in an executive's life," notes Karen Ganzlin. "You have to sleep on things, clear your head, and sometimes you have to make a decision with a not-great list of choices. I end up talking to myself and self-reflecting a lot when I run five miles every night. You'd be amazed what I work out in those five-mile runs."

On Self-Review

"Early on, my first major job was working in Texas. I was hired by the president of the company, who had a particularly blunt, direct style. We learned to work well together and I began taking the same approach with others in the company that I did with him. On the day of my performance review with the COO, I thought to myself, "I'm in for a terrific review." The first thing the COO told me was that the president loved me. He then contrasted that by saying that everyone else didn't think I was a good team member. Here I was using the harsh, direct style that worked well with the president with everyone. I thought, 'How could I be so blind?' We're all experts when looking at the past though. I see now that I would have been more successful if I really looked around at the culture and the way people related."

—Linda Descano, president and CEO of Women & Co., a program of Citibank

The conversation that happens with yourself when you reflect is enlightening. You can get yourself in the habit of asking questions such as, "How did I feel in that meeting? Did I maximize my talents today? Have I challenged myself fully to solve this problem?" Doing so is a hallmark of a leader.

A terrific compass you can use throughout your career is right under your nose. "Stay anchored in your own personal values," advises Karen Ganzlin. "That will help you decipher what's really important so there's no mismatch." Knowing our personal values helps us not go against ourselves or live someone else's expectation of us. Lori Greenawalt talked about this trap, saying, "So often we try to live someone else's career, not our own. In the case of some of my colleagues, they'd been reading the *Wall Street Journal* every day with their dad since they were ten, when I didn't even know what it was. Sometimes we get tied up in 'It's not fair that they got this advantage and I didn't.' Don't worry so much about everyone else. Find a trajectory and live your own career."

BECAUSE NO ONE ELSE WILL DO IT FOR YOU . . .

Part of taking total ownership over our careers is seeing that technical skills are one small part of how we can make an impact. What we'll become known for is made up of far more than our smarts. "There's so much I wish I knew sooner but the single most important thing is that doing good work isn't enough," recalls Lori A. Greenawalt. "I've looked back a hundred times and realized consistent hard work is just a platform on which you build the rest of your career. Good work is a foundational piece, so your company knows what they'll get every day, but there's so much more to advancing. Understanding politics, smart navigation, strategic thinking, and driving your own career are what I realized later were equally as important."

If there's one central theme that's been woven throughout this book, it's *self-directed action.* No one else is going to build those relationships for you, no one else is going to shape your personal brand, and certainly no one else will advocate on your behalf for what you truly want. Taking complete responsibility for the results we have today reminds us of the active role we play in our future and overall well-being. Irene Chang Britt says it best when she notes, "We have to know that we're responsible for the results we create. We're victors, not victims. A mind-set of personal responsibility is really important."

As you think about who you are now and who you have yet to grow into, don't let your own potential frighten you. You have the power of self-advocacy now, and you'll have even more of it in the future. You can—without a doubt—find fulfilling work, have the self-confidence to speak your mind, and invent options for yourself that don't yet exist. You have thousands of times the strength, nerve, and resolve that you think you do.

In the end, your career and your life are all about choices. Not asking is a choice, asking and acquiescing to something you hate is a choice, and surely, asking and getting what you want represents a choice. As the next generation of women leaders, we're hungry for choices. We're hungry for change. Luckily, the timing and conditions are perfect and the world desperately needs your input, your involvement, your leadership.

You know how to push back and now it's time to put those skills to work. Asking will change your life, open up the world in ways you never thought possible, and free your relationships from unspoken burdens. Asking also cascades well beyond us. After all, what better legacy can we leave our daughters, nieces, sisters, and friends than to go get what we want?

Notes

PREFACE

1. U.S. Census Bureau, "Table 587: Foreign-Born and Native-Born Populations—Employment Status by Selected Characteristics, 2009," *Labor Force, Employment, and Earnings, U.S. Census Bureau, Statistical Abstract of the United States: 2011* (2011). http://www.census.gov/prod/2011pubs/11statab/labor.pdf.

2. National Center for Education Statistics, "Table 269: First-Professional Degrees Conferred by Degree-Granting Institutions in Dentistry, Medicine, and Law, by Number of Institutions Conferring Degrees and Sex of Student: Selected Years, 1949–50 Through 2005–06," *Digest of Education Statistics* (2007). http://nces.ed.gov/programs/digest/d07/tables/dt07_269.asp. National Center for Education Statistics, "Table 264: Bachelor's, Master's, and Doctor's Degrees Conferred by Degree-Granting Institutions, by Field of Study and Year: Selected Years, 1970–71 Through 2005–06," *Digest of Education Statistics* (2007). http://nces.ed.gov/programs/digest /d07/tables/dt07_264.asp.

3. Michael J. Silverstein, Kate Sayre, and John Butman, *Women Want More: How to Capture Your Share of the World's Largest, Fastest-Growing Market* (New York: Harper Collins, 2009), 221.

Chapter 1: Why Push Back?

1. Linda Babcock and Sara Laschever, "Interesting Statistics," *Women Don't Ask: Negotiation and the Gender Divide* (n.d.). www.womendontask.com/stats.html.

2. U.S. Census Bureau (2011).

3. National Center for Education Statistics, "Table 264" (2007).

4. M. Robyn Andersen, Janne Abullrade, and Nicole Urban, "Assertiveness with Physicians Is Related to Women's Perceived Roles in the Medical Encounter," *Women & Health, 42,* no. 2 (2005), 15–33.

5. Linda Babcock and Sara Laschever, *Women Don't Ask: Negotiation and the Gender Divide* (Princeton: Princeton University Press, 2003), 125–126.

6. Georges Desvaux, Sandrine Devillard-Hoellinger, and Mary C. Meaney, "A Business Case for Women," *The McKinsey Quarterly* (September 2008), 4.

7. National Committee on Pay, *The Wage Gap over Time: In Real Dollars, Women See a Continuing Gap* (September 2011). www .pay-equity.org/info-time.html.

8. Michael Peterson, "What Men and Women Value at Work: Implications for Workplace Health," *Gender Medicine: The Journal for the Study of Sex & Gender Differences, 1,* no. 2 (December 2004), 106–124, doi: 10.1016/S1550–8579(04)80016–0.

9. Lois Frankel, *Nice Girls Don't Get Rich: 75 Avoidable Mistakes Women Make with Money* (New York: Business Plus, 2005), 14.

10. Michael J. Silverstein, Kate Sayre, and John Butman, *Women Want More: How to Capture Your Share of the World's Largest, Fastest-Growing Market* (New York: Harper Collins, 2009), 282.

11. National Committee on Pay (September 2011).

12. Manisha Thakor and Sharon Kedar, *On My Own Two Feet: A Modern Girl's Guide to Personal Finance* (Avon, MA: Adams Business, 2007), xii.

13. Jeffrey R. Lewis and Cindy Hounsell, *What Women Need to Know About Retirement: A Joint Project of the Heinz Family Philanthropies and The Women's Institute for a Secure Retirement* (Washington, DC: Heinz Family Philanthropies and The Women's Institute for a Secure Retirement, 2011), 3.

14. Jody Heymann, Alison Earle, and Jeffrey Hayes, *The Work, Family, and Equity Index: How Does the United States Measure Up?* (Montreal: The Institute for Health and Social Policy at McGill University, 2007), 1. www.mcgill.ca/files/ihsp/WFEIFinal2007.pdf.

15. Accenture, *2010 Women's Research—Millennial Women in the Workplace Success Index: Striving for Balance.* (2010). www.accenture.com/Global/About_Accenture/Company_Overview/Our_People/Women_at_Accenture/Research/Striving-for-Balance.htm.

16. Willow Bay, "What a Generation Y Woman Really Wants?" *Huffington Post* (March 23, 2007). www.huffingtonpost.com/willow-bay/what-a-generation-y-woman_b_44132.html.

17. Sylvia Ann Hewlett, Maggie Jackson, Laura Sherbin, Peggy Shiller, Eytan Sosnovich, and Karen Sumberg, *Bookend Generations: Leveraging Talent and Finding Common Ground* (New York: Center for Work-Life Policy, 2009).

18. Daniel Goleman, *Working with Emotional Intelligence* (New York: Bantam Books, 1998), 7.

CHAPTER 2: FIND YOUR PUSHBACK STYLE

1. U.S. Census Bureau (2011).

2. Eric J. Mash and Russell A. Barkley, *Child Psychopathology* (2nd ed.) (New York: The Guilford Press, 2003), 14.

3. Julie E. Phelan, Corinne A. Moss-Racusin, and Laurie A. Rudman, "Competent Yet out in the Cold: Shifting Criteria for Hiring Reflect Backlash Toward Agentic Women," *Psychology of Women Quarterly, 32* (2008), 406–413.

4. Catalyst Organization, *Women "Take Care," Men "Take Charge": Stereotyping of U.S. Business Leaders Exposed.* (October 2005). www.catalyst.org/publication/94/women-take-care-men -take-charge-stereotyping-of-us-business-leaders-exposed.

5. Albert Bandura, *Self-Efficacy in Changing Societies* (Cambridge, UK: Cambridge University Press, 1995), 11.

6. Catherine Hill, Christianne Corbett, and Andresse St. Rose, *Why So Few? Women in Science, Technology, Engineering, and Mathematics* (Washington, DC: American Association of University Women, 2010).

7. Carol Dweck, "Is Math a Gift? Beliefs That Put Females at Risk," in S. J. Ceci and W. M. Williams (eds.), *Why Aren't More Women in Science? Top Researchers Debate the Evidence* (Washington, DC: American Psychological Association, 2006), 47–55. Carol Dweck, *Mindsets and Math/Science Achievement*

(New York: Carnegie Corporation of New York, Institute for Advanced Study, Commission on Mathematics and Science Education, 2008). Carol Dweck and Ellen L. Leggett, "A Social-Cognitive Approach to Motivation and Personality," *Psychological Review, 95,* no. 2 (1988), 256–273.

8. TED Talks, *Sheryl Sandberg: Why We Have Too Few Women Leaders.* (December 2010). www.ted.com/talks/sheryl _sandberg_why_we_have_too_few_women_leaders.html.

CHAPTER 3: PREPARE PSYCHOLOGICALLY

1. Noraini M. Noor, "Work-Family Conflict, Locus of Control, and Women's Well-Being: Tests of Alternative Pathways," *The Journal of Social Psychology, 142*, no. 5 (2002), 645–662.

2. Linda Babcock and Sara Laschever (2003).

3. Alex Pentland, "How Social Networks Network Best," *Harvard Business Review* (2009). http://hbr.org/web/2009/hbr-list/how -social-networks-work-best.

4. Martha Lagace, "Negotiating Challenges for Women Leaders. Q&A with Kathleen L. McGinn," *Working Knowledge* (October 13, 2003). http://hbswk.hbs.edu/item/3711.html.

5. Peggy Klaus, *The Art of Tooting Your Own Horn Without Blowing It* (New York: Warner Business, 2004), 16.

6. Wayne H. Bylsma and Brenda Major, "Social Comparisons and Contentment: Exploring the Psychological Costs of the Gender Wage Gap," *Psychology of Women Quarterly, 18*, no. 2 (June 1994), 241–249. DOI: 10.1111/j.1471-6402.1994.tb00453.x.

7. The Harvard Negotiation Project, *The Angry Negotiator* (November 22, 2010). www.pon.harvard.edu/daily/negotiation -skills-daily/the-angry-negotiator/.

8. The Harvard Negotiation Project (2010).

9. The Happiness Institute. *Happiness Is . . . Learning from Aikido* (April 26, 2011). www.thehappinessinstitute.com/blog/article .aspx?c=3&a=2896.

Chapter 4: Do Your Homework

1. Ed Wallace, *Business Relationships That Last: Five Steps to Transform Contacts into High-Performing Relationships* (Austin, TX: Greenleaf Book Group, 2009), 3.

2. Sylvia Ann Hewlett, with Kerrie Peraino, Laura Sherbin, and Karen Sumberg, "The Sponsor Effect: Breaking Through the Last Glass Ceiling," *Harvard Business Review Research Report* (December 2010). http://cpradr.org/Portals/0/Committees /Industry%20Committees/National%20Task%20Force%20on %20Diversity%20in%20ADR/Materials/The%20Sponsor %20Effect%20-%20Breaking%20Through%20the%20Last %20Glass%20Ceiling.pdf

3. The Harvard Negotiation Project. *Dealing with Busy People* (April 25, 2011). www.pon.harvard.edu/daily/negotiation-skills -daily/dealing-with-busy-people/?mqsc=E04/26/117:30AM.

4. Peter Guber, *Tell to Win: Connect, Persuade, and Triumph with the Hidden Power of Story* (New York: Crown Business Books, 2011), 16.

5. The OpEd Project, 2011. *Basic Op-Ed Structure.* www
   .theopedproject.org/index.php?option=com_content&view
   =article&id=68&Itemid=80.

6. Michelle Lynn Smith, *The Forgotten Middle Child of Memory:
   The Serial Position Effect* (Murfreesboro: Middle Tennessee State
   University, 2011). http://frank.mtsu.edu/~sschmidt/Cognitive
   /sample_report.htm.

7. Christie Nicholson, "Business, Lies and E-mail," *Scientific
   American* (September 29, 2008). www.scientificamerican.com
   /podcast/episode.cfm?id=business-lies-and-e-mail-08–09–29.

8. Neil Schoenherr, *Playing Hardball in Negotiations: Home
   Field Provides Advantage* (Washington University in St. Louis
   online, April 8, 2011). http://news.wustl.edu/news/Pages
   /22150.aspx.

CHAPTER 5: MANEUVERING THROUGH THE CONVERSATION

1. Adam D. Galinsky, "Should You Make the First Offer?"
   Negotiation, 7, no. 7 (July 2004), 1–4.

2. Ibid.

3. Ibid.

4. Negotiation Space, *Walk a Mile in Someone Else's Shoes* (April
   27, 2011). www.karrass.com/blog/walk-a-mile-in-someone
   -elses-shoes/.

5. Galinsky (2004).

6. Chester L. Karrass, *Give and Take* (rev. ed.) (New York: Harper
   Collins, 1993), 38.

7. Richard Shell, "Three Assumptions That Undermine Your
    Success," *International Business Times* (April 7, 2011).
    http://hken.ibtimes.com/articles/131464/20110407/executive
    -negotiation-workshop-wharton-business-school.htm.

Chapter 6: Follow Up

1. Linda Babcock and Sara Laschever, *Ask for It: How Women Can
    Use the Power of Negotiation to Get What They Really Want*
    (New York: Bantam Books, 2008), 284.

Acknowledgments

So many women helped me to create this book, starting with the twenty executives I sat down with and interviewed, each of whom I've come to adopt as a mentor. Truly candid interviews—in which subjects share their most agonizing mistakes, hardest-won successes, even their prickly regrets—are hard to come by. And yet, that frankness, in the spirit of helping young women, is exactly what these women bestowed.

The all-girl brigade at DSM Agency in New York was instrumental in making the book, which started out as a far-away daydream, into the real thing. Doris S. Michaels, my agent and a savvy businesswoman herself, had faith in my concept, a conviction that strengthened my resolve and fueled my writing throughout the project. Thanks are also in order for the contributions of the razor-sharp and supportive Delia Berrigan Fakis and Michelle Wegenstein at DSM, who helped me shape the right tone and tenor for the book.

How lucky I was to be match-made with Jossey-Bass as a publisher and in particular, Genoveva Llosa, the most exceptional editor out there. Aside from being tactful, generous, committed, and insightful, Genoveva held me accountable to my original vision of the book, improving my manuscript with every piece of feedback she proffered. To work with her again would be a dream.

Much of the work of a writer requires solitude. Imagine my surprise at finding an extensive, engaged, and loyal community, online and offline, who cheered me from the sidelines and inspired me with their work to advance women. My thanks to 85 Broads, The Forté Foundation, The Glass Hammer, the National Association of Women MBAs, Caroline Howard and the ForbesWoman crew, Lily Cunningham at the *Washington Post*, SheShouldRun, No Country for Young Women, She Negotiates, Catalyst, GetRaised, the Women's Media Center, Kathy Korman Frey, Lisa Weinert, Jody Glickman, Manisha Thakor, Nina Godiwalla, Deirdre Joy Smith, Susan G. Bell, Tre Rodriguez, and Whitney Gray Wilkerson.

Many a friend and family member have suffered my writing pains with love, understanding, and humor. Thank you to my Johns Hopkins brigade and to Pari and the rest of my peer-coaching posse for encouraging me. My unending love to every one of the Khans and Rezvanis, to Emily, Tanya, Leslie, Mary, Anne, Megan, Julie, Nina, Shannon, Jane, Rosanne, Omar, and Mimi. You have my bottomless respect, appreciation, and allegiance.

And to Geoff Rezvani, my universe.

About the Author

Selena Rezvani is a recognized authority on women and leadership and is a leading author, speaker, and consultant regarding women and the workplace. She is the co-owner of Women's Roadmap, a consulting firm that elevates women into leadership through assessment, the design of gender-inclusive policies, and coaching. Outside of her consulting and coaching work, Selena promotes her message through training programs, teaching some of the brightest minds in business at Harvard, SAP, Princeton, Comcast, UBS, Duke, Johnson & Johnson, and many others.

Her experience and success in the women and leadership arena make Rezvani a frequent resource for news media. She has been quoted, interviewed, and profiled by CareerBuilder, the *Wall Street Journal, Forbes,* ABC, and NBC. She is a regular commentator on NPR's syndicated *51 Percent: The Women's Perspective* and writes columns on women and leadership for the *Washington Post* and *Forbes.* She is the author of the book *The Next Generation of Women Leaders: What You Need to Lead but Won't Learn in Business School* (Praeger, 2009).

Selena received her bachelor of science and master of social work degrees from New York University, and has an MBA from Johns Hopkins University, where she was the recipient of the Edward Stegman Award for academic excellence. She lives near Philadelphia.

Index